BEOWULF'S
ECSTATIC TRANCE
MAGIC

"Here Brink returns with his lively combination of ancestral imagination, mythology, and historical reality, applying it this time to the oldest known epic poem written in the English language. Again referring to a series of ecstatic trance postures that have been identified elsewhere as having ancient use for facilitating a variety of meditative inquiries, the book becomes a detailed, novel-length account of the author's own ecstatic trance journeys into the story of Beowulf. The author, as he should, leaves the reader to form his or her own opinion as to the degree to which the amplifications of the story can be taken literally or as metaphor, as reality or imaginal fantasy, as personal or collective. As James Hillman suggested, imagination and soul are fundamentally the same thing, and in that sense this book is another soul-focused journey into some of the long ago roots of modern civilization."

RAYMOND HILLIS, PH.D.,
PROFESSOR EMERITUS OF COUNSELING,
CALIFORNIA STATE UNIVERSITY, LOS ANGELES

"Brink presents an interesting system of inducing trance by means of ritual postures and uses it to present an imaginative look at an Anglo-Saxon legend."

ALICE KARLSDÓTTIR,
AUTHOR OF *NORSE GODDESS MAGIC*

Wealhtheow's tapestry of a ship with a line of men at the oars.

BEOWULF'S
ECSTATIC TRANCE
MAGIC

Accessing the Archaic Powers
of the Universal Mind

NICHOLAS E. BRINK, PH.D.

Bear & Company
Rochester, Vermont • Toronto, Canada

Bear & Company
One Park Street
Rochester, Vermont 05767
www.BearandCompanyBooks.com

Bear & Company is a division of Inner Traditions International

Library of Congress Cataloging-in-Publication Data
Brink, Nicholas E., 1939-
  Beowulf's ecstatic trance magic : accessing the archaic powers of the universal
mind / Nicholas E. Brink, Ph.D.
      pages cm
  Includes bibliographical references and index.
  Summary: "Use ecstatic trance to journey to the time of Beowulf and learn first
hand the ancient magic of the early Nordic people"-- Provided by publisher.
  ISBN 978-1-59143-217-3 (pbk.) — ISBN 978-1-59143-218-0 (e-book)
  1. Beowulf. 2. Magic in literature. 3. Magic—Scandinavia—History. 4. Trance.
5. Epic poetry, English (Old)—History and criticism. I. Title.
  PR1585.B66 2016
  829'.3—dc23
                                                                  2015016798

Printed and bound in the United States by Lake Book Manufacturing, Inc.
The text stock is SFI certified. The Sustainable Forestry Initiative® program
promotes sustainable forest management.

10 9 8 7 6 5 4 3 2 1

Text design and layout by Virginia Scott Bowman
This book was typeset in Garamond Premier Pro and Gill Sans with Bougan Black
    and Gill Sans used as display typefaces
Artwork by M. J. Ruhe

To send correspondence to the author of this book, mail a first-class letter to the
author c/o Inner Traditions • Bear & Company, One Park Street, Rochester, VT
05767, and we will forward the communication, or contact the author directly at
www.imaginalmind.net.

CONTENTS

FOREWORD

STANLEY KRIPPNER, PH.D.

Beowulf is the oldest surviving epic poem written in Old English; however, the story is set in Scandinavia, not England. It relates how the warrior Beowulf comes to the aid of a Danish king named Hrothgar. The king's great hall has been attacked by Grendel, a monster whose peace has been disturbed by revelry in the hall; the creature has killed members of the royal court in reprisal for this transgression. Beowulf mortally wounds the monster, but his work is not finished because Grendel's equally horrendous mother strikes back in revenge. Beowulf tracks her down in the monsters' underwater lair and destroys her as well.

In *Beowulf's Ecstatic Trance Magic,* Nicholas Brink focuses on King Hrothgar's wife, Queen Wealhtheow, and her *guvernante,* her teacher, Vanadisdottir. Before becoming queen, Wealhtheow was raised under the tutelage of Vanadisdottir, a priestess of the goddess Freyja, and Wealhtheow's mother before her worshiped this Scandinavian Mother Goddess as well. As a result of this upbringing, Wealhtheow is an advocate of peace and compassion, which does not resonate with her husband's warrior lifestyle. As a result, she understands why Grendel was annoyed by Hrothgar's men's wild, drunken behavior, and her compassion puts her at odds with her husband.

These traits of Queen Wealhtheow are not described in the epic poem *Beowulf,* and so how does Brink know this? He uses shamanic methods to go back in time—specifically, using ecstatic trance.

Traditionally shamans have taken their legendary journeys to other worlds with the aid of percussion instruments (usually drums), chanting, and mental imagery, and by assuming specific postures. Brink used ecstatic trance to write an earlier book, *Baldr's Magic,* and this serves him well in this work too. The author adopted a daily routine that involved putting himself into a shamanic posture and allowing the journey to begin. In doing this he found himself in one of two locations, in Sweden or Denmark, places that he had visited previously in physical travel.

Brink's shamanic journeys took him into a distant time in the past—the era of Beowulf and the Scandinavian epic that he knows quite well. It was a time when the hunter-gatherer era was giving way to settlements and kingdoms, and with that, territorial disputes. Along with this paradigm shift, the veneration of a peaceful and nurturing Mother Goddess was losing its grip to a new set of patriarchal, warring gods. Harmony was giving way to conflict, collaboration to rivalry. Brink proposes that the present turmoil on Earth is a continuation of these earlier disruptions, and that a return to the values of an earlier epoch is humankind's best chance for survival.

The readers of this marvelously prescient work will be entertained by the mythological saga as it unfolds. At the same time they will see reflections of the ancient past in contemporary crises. Hence, *Beowulf's Ecstatic Trance Magic* can be read for the sheer enjoyment of its romances, wars, and intrigues, as well as being appreciated as a blueprint for humanity's emergence from its current morass into a benevolent new world, one in which Queen Wealhtheow and Vanadisdottir would feel at home.

STANLEY KRIPPNER, Ph.D., is a professor of psychology at Saybrook University and past president of the Association for Humanistic Psychology. The recipient of several distinguished awards and author and coauthor of many books, including *Demystifying Shamans and Their World,* he lives in San Rafael, California.

ACKNOWLEDGMENTS

Each day while using ecstatic trance I call upon the spirits of the Earth to hear what they have to say. What they have said has become this book; thus I dedicate this book to these spirits.

"Who are these spirits?" you may ask. The spirits with which you are most familiar are the ones you have met at night in your dreams. Every character or spirit in your dreams has a message for you. I call upon the spirits of each direction as well as the spirit of the posture I use. These spirits guided my experience by providing the spirit characters and the story of this book. These spirits may sometimes come from the unconscious mind, but also from beyond, from the universal mind. All, in their wisdom, deserve great respect and honor.

Journeying back from the extrasensory world of the spirits to the world I perceive with my five senses, I also thank Martha Ruhe, the artist/illustrator for this book, Meghan MacLean, the project editor, and the staff of Bear & Co. who put so much effort into making this book fit to print.

A SHIFT ON OUR PLANET

Something major is happening on planet Earth. There are those who predict that Earth as we know Her is coming to an end, proclaiming that climate change and the spread of radiation from the 2011 Fukushima nuclear disaster are now unstoppable. There are also those who deny this end of our world as we've known it, who are hanging on for dear life to their consuming, capitalistic ways, resisting any change or progressive thinking. As these two forces clash, they bring great turmoil to this planet. I see this chaos and turmoil as the death throes of an old age and the dawning of a new one. Some of us, though, qualify this prediction with the statement *if we don't destroy ourselves first.*

In his groundbreaking work *The Ever-Present Origin,* philosopher, linguist, and poet Jean Gebser argues that the structure of human consciousness—the way in which we look at the world—has mutated through four distinct eras, and that we are now entering a fifth era of consciousness. Following the first era, the archaic era, characterized by zero-dimensional or nonindividuated consciousness, came the second era, the magical era of the hunter-gatherers. The third era began about 10,000 years ago in the area we now refer to as the Near East. This was a time when humans sought ways to mythically explain why things are the way they are; it was also the era when humans began farming and domesticating animals—that is, when they began their quest to control the earth. Yet because of the onset of the relatively recent Ice Age and the ice's gradual retreat northward, this era was considerably shorter in

Scandinavia, where the story of the legendary warrior Beowulf unfolds.

The mythic era was followed by 2,500 years of rational consciousness, of seeking to explain the world through scientific methodology and empiricism. This fourth era, known as the mental era, has led to the innumerable ways that we now attempt to control our environment—ways that are bringing us closer to our species' extinction.

Gebser posits that we are now entering a fifth era, the integral era, which he says is characterized by time-free transparency. This era goes beyond the rational, linear, three-dimensional world and is taking us into the fourth dimension, where time and space is relative. Time-free transparency means to see transparently the essential quality of something outside of or free of the constraints of time and space. Throughout our current, mental era we considered the magical ways of the earlier era as irrational and superstitious; but now in the emerging era of time-free transparency we can perceive the essence of the magic of the second era; that is, it becomes transparent to us. This emerging fifth era opens us to a deeper understanding of the magical powers of the second era, powers that we now realize are real and powerful in sustaining life. The title of Gebser's book, *The Ever-Present Origin,* reflects this transparency and reconnection with our origins in the interdependence with all the magic and enchantment of Earth, with all that is animate and inanimate, which we depend on and which depends on us.

Beowulf's Ecstatic Trance Magic is about rediscovering this original magic and how it is part of this new age as we reconnect with our great Mother Earth. Many writers, including Barbara Hand Clow, Richard Tarnas, Carl Johan Calleman, and Sergio Magaña, to name a few, offer us their vision of this emerging new age. Barbara Hand Clow sees a world of peace inhabited by *Homo pacem,* a species focused on peace. Richard Tarnas has the hope that we will rediscover the world soul, or *anima mundi,* and will no longer feel separated from the enchantment of Earth but at one with it. Carl Calleman describes this new era as one in which we will find unity, freeing us from the conflicts caused by dualistic thinking.

In *Dawn of the Akashic Age,* integral theorist Ervin Laszlo and researcher Kingsley L. Dennis offer a broader picture of this new world, a world where people everywhere will be able to communicate telepathically. They will insist on peace, and capitalism will disappear as cooperatives or worker-owned businesses arise to take its place. Education will evolve, with each person pursuing his or her own interests, unique from the interests of others, thus making us dependent on one another in order to access the broad wealth of knowledge available to us. Laszlo and Dennis believe that the turmoil of the present period of transition will continue until 2020, unless we destroy ourselves first; after that, it will become very apparent that we have attained this new age.

Sergio Magaña, a Nahuatl shaman, sees the prophetic signs of us attaining the knowledge of Mother Earth and her cycles[1] by learning to remember and interpret our sleeping and waking dreams.[2] We will "come to know the beauty and harmony" of ancient Mexico, he says.[3] Magaña sees that this new world will be rooted in our ancient past. Both Magaña and Gebser recognize that these changes will occur only through great turmoil and chaos. In the words of Magaña, the old ways of the ancients "will resurrect amidst whirlwind emotional currents and burning flames of light."[4] Likewise, according to Gebser, the transitions between eras

are times of disturbance and even destruction. The fact that a given vessel—in this case man—is compelled or enabled to realize an additional possibility, an additional possibility of the world, causes first of all a shake-up of the previously existing, habitual vital-psychic-mental order. The resultant disorder, if it is not mastered on the strength of insight into the occurring mutation, brings on chaos rather than a restructuration and novel constellation of reality. . . . The tendency toward chaos, decay, decline, disruption; the loss and renunciation of once legitimate values; and the rise of the devalued and worthless, which are all prominent expressions of our epoch, present major obstacles to the interpretation of manifestations of the consciousness.[5]

I find that there are two sources of knowledge needed for the emerging age of time-free transparency. The first comes from the hunter-gatherer cultures, some of which still exist today, cultures that have been studied extensively by anthropologists. Stories that show the powers of contemporary shamans of North America were collected by Native American author, theologian, historian, and activist Vine Deloria and recorded in his last book, *The World We Used to Live In,* prior to his death in 2005. These stories show us the power of ecstatic trance, powers that each of us can cultivate and possess in the emerging age. The second source of knowledge can be found in what we can gain from ancient cultures as is done in dreaming, both while sleeping and while awake, in ecstatic trance. My most recent book, *Baldr's Magic: The Power of Norse Shamanism and Ecstatic Trance,* used both hypnosis and ecstatic trance to access this ancient world; this book accesses it solely through ecstatic trance posture work.

Many of the rational, linear thinkers of the mental era of consciousness do not believe that this ancient world can be accessed in these ways, yet there is considerable research being done and evidence that demonstrates that this is indeed possible. This research also explores the mechanisms of how this magic works. These investigators include Rupert Sheldrake, Ervin Laszlo, Dean Radin, and Gregg Braden, among others. Radin, the director of research at the Institute of Noetic Sciences, has reviewed a large number of research studies of mental telepathy and psychokinesis, studies that demonstrate the reality of these powers with extremely high levels of statistical significance. The research of Sheldrake, a biochemist and cell biologist who has done extensive research and writing on the subject of parapsychology, suggests that if the universe is held together by gravitational fields, and the atom by electromagnetic fields, since our body is composed of these atoms each cell of our body has its own field. Sheldrake calls them *morphic fields.* Extending this thinking further, he says that each organ of our body has its own morphic field, as does our whole body. The body's morphic field unites with the fields of all other human beings, whose fields in turn similarly unite with each of the other species of life on Earth, in the same way that multiple gravitational fields unite the universe. Sheldrake believes that these morphic fields contain stored information, information about everything that has happened since the beginning of time. Ervin Laszlo, a philosopher of science, systems analyst, and integral theorist, has named these fields of information *Akashic fields.* He describes them as holographic matrices of information that can be accessed anywhere, at any time. He also suggests that we have sensory receptors that perceive this information: the cytoskeletal structure of the brain that is composed of 10^{18} microtubules.[6] Bestselling author and New Age thinker Gregg Braden refers to these information fields as the Divine Matrix.

Much of this current research relies on the theories of modern or quantum physics. One of these theories is that of nonlocal coherence— that matter or energy waves, when split, share the same state, which remains interlinked forever, no matter how far in time and space the waves may be from one another. Related to this is the theory of the relativity of time, which says that when subatomic particles collide, some particles may go backward in time and thus can provide information about the future. It is this understanding that gave Gebser the description of this new, fifth era of consciousness, that of time-free transparency.[7]

Accessing this information field, which I call the Universal Mind, is facilitated by altered states of consciousness. In my work I have relied on three different ways to attain an altered state: dreaming, hypnosis, and ecstatic trance. Through these methods I have explored the lives of the hunter-gatherers and of those subsequent people who lived during the transition to farming and the domestication of animals. Central to both ecstatic trance and hypnosis is the ability to pay attention to one's center of harmony with an attitude of patience, gentleness, and curiosity.

The center of harmony, which lies just below the umbilicus, is the *dant'ian,* the center of energy in t'ai chi. It is the dwelling place of rest, the place where we feel at ease. Attending to the center of harmony, our abdomen rises and falls with each in-breath and out-breath, initiating trance by calming our thoughts. This practice, when accompanied by the rapid beating of the drum (as in ecstatic trance) or the pacing of words (in the case of hypnosis) in sync with the listener's breathing is part of inducing trance or an altered state of consciousness. In hypnosis, the spoken words assist the induction of trance when they validate the experience and thinking of the listener; these words are those to which the listener can answer "yes, that is what I am thinking or feeling"—in other words, they create what is known as a *yes-set*. Inducing ecstatic trance is different. The rapid beating of a drum distracts us from our interfering thoughts. But as we stand, sit, or lie in specific postures, postures that define the intent of our journey, they bring us into a state of ecstatic trance. Dreaming also brings us into an altered state of consciousness, especially when we fall asleep with a specific intent, such as asking our dreams to give us a gift or answer some question. When within a dream we realize we are dreaming, the dream can then be considered lucid, such that we can pursue the answers to questions in that exceptional state.

All three of these altered states, each different in some ways, can each bring us to a point where we can experience the magic, or *seiðr* (pronounced *sathe,* as in the word *bathe*), of ancient times as practiced by a growing number of people around the world who hold the dream of world peace and contentment. These altered states can bring us in contact with our ancestors, with our past lives, with people who live now, and with our great Mother Earth. They bring us into an extrasensory telepathic awareness of what each knows and thinks, of how each lives. These altered states bring us into deeper communion with all that is around us, past and present, into a deeper understanding, an understanding that brings us to a new sense of well-being.

Using the altered state of ecstatic trance, this book takes us back to the life of Queen Wealhtheow, the consort of King Hrothgar in the ancient epic poem *Beowulf,* the oldest piece of literature written in the English language.* This epic story likely takes place in the latter half of

*I have used David Wright's 1957 translation of *Beowulf.*

the sixth century CE. It tells of a time of power and strength, of men in conquest of lands that would increase the territory of kings, yet also of a time when some would remember the stories of an earlier matriarchal era, a magical time of peace and nurturance. I have used ecstatic trance to return to this ancient time, a time of transition from the magical era to the mythic era of consciousness, to uncover the magic, or seiðr, of the early Nordic people.

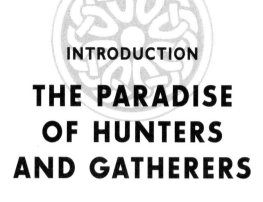

THE PARADISE
OF HUNTERS
AND GATHERERS

For about 200,000 years, we *Homo sapiens* wandered the earth hunting and gathering in the Garden of Eden. Our wandering began in Central East Africa and gradually spread to eventually reach all corners of the earth. My own genetic line wandered north into Scandinavia. Genetic tests have revealed to me that I have a gene that is possessed by over 50 percent of the Sami reindeer herders of Finland. Life during those earlier times is succinctly described by American anthrolpologist Felicitas Goodman:

> In a very real way, the hunters and gatherers open the first chapter of our human history. And fittingly, this dawning was as close to paradise as humans have ever been able to achieve. The men did the hunting and scavenging, working for about three hours a week, and the women took care of daily sustenance by gathering vegetal food and small animals. It was such a harmonious existence, such a successful adaptation, that it did not materially alter for many thousands of years. This view is not romanticizing matters. Those hunter-gatherer societies that have survived into the present still pursue the same lifestyle, and we are quite familiar with it from

contemporary anthropological observation. Despite the unavoidable privations of human existence, despite occasional hunger, illness, and other trials, what makes their lifeways so enviable is the fact that knowing every nook and cranny of their home territory and all that grows and lives in it, the bands make their regular rounds and take only what they need. By modern calculations, that amounts to only about 10 percent of the yield, easily recoverable under undisturbed conditions. They live a life of total balance, because *they do not aspire to controlling their habitat, they are a part of it.*[1]

Yet for about the last 10,000 years, as human beings became agriculturists and domesticators of animals, our increased pillaging and destruction of the earth has led us to where we find ourselves today. We have created a religion that tells us that we were thrown out of the Garden of Eden because of our knowledge of good and evil, and that we are to have dominion over the earth. We have defined ourselves as superior to every other creature, the culmination of evolution. We have separated and isolated ourselves from that which sustains us, from the great Mother Earth. We are now at a critical moment in time when what has sustained us is close to being gone. Our survival depends on our reconnecting with and learning from those civilizations that venerated Mother Earth in her sustaining capacity. We must end our dependence on fossil fuels and other "natural resources" that we take from her belly. Hopefully it is not too late to do so. These hunter-gatherer civilizations have much to teach us, both those that still exist today and those that existed in our ancient past. Most important, we have ways to access their ways of life so we can learn how to survive the current crises on Earth.

The magic of the life of the hunter-gatherer can be retrieved by recreating their ecstatic ways, their ways of healing, of connecting with the spirits of their ancestors and the spirits of the land, and of being one with the Earth. These ways begin with the induction of ecstatic trance through stimulation of the nervous system with the rapid beat of a drum. Ecstatic trance is a skill that has become available to us as a result of the pioneering research of anthropologist Felicitas Goodman, as well as others. It is a skill of the shamans of our ancient and present-day hunter-gatherer societies, a skill we all can learn. There are groups of people throughout the world who have been learning and practicing this skill. As a result of my training at the Cuyamungue Institute with psychologist and coach Belinda Gore, a close friend and colleague of Felicitas Goodman, I have become a certified instructor of ecstatic trance.

Through ecstatic trance I have discovered that I can extrasensorally and telepathically experience what others are experiencing; I can facilitate healing, and I can spirit journey in ways others have not experienced. In this journeying I have gone back to be with my distant ancestors, as described in my most recent book, *Baldr's Magic: The Power of Norse Shamanism and Ecstatic Trance*. Now, in this book, I journey back in time to be with Queen Wealhtheow, whose story is the subject of *Beowulf*. In these ecstatic trance journeys I feel that I am making a connection with the ancestral spirits of the land and not my specific ancestors, yet I feel especially connected to three shamans who are part of this story: Vanadisdottir, Forsetason, and Healfdall. This story feels very real to me as I experienced it in the altered state of ecstatic trance, a trance state that continued as I sat to record the experiences—they again became very alive and vivid to me.

In my previous two books, *The Power of Ecstatic Trance: Practices for Healing, Spiritual Growth, and Accessing the Universal Mind* and *Baldr's Magic,* I describe in considerable detail the ways of ecstatic trance and specific shamanic postures. Some of these postures are used for journeying into the underworld, the middle world, and the upper world. Other postures are for the purposes of divination, for healing, for metamorphosis or shape-shifting, and for initiation or the experience of death and rebirth. In her many years of anthropological research, Felicitas Goodman studied the art of both ancient and contemporary hunter-gatherer peoples and identified what she believed were the postures used by the shamans of those peoples. She wrote of her research in her book *Where the Spirits Ride the Wind: Trance Journeys and Other Ecstatic Experiences.* Dr. Goodman's colleague Belinda Gore has written two books cataloging these postures: *Ecstatic Body Postures: An Alternate Reality Workbook* and *The Ecstatic Experience: Healing Postures for Spirit Journeys.** In this book I add only one new posture, which is described in chapter 22; it is called the Højby Middle World posture that was found near Højby, Denmark and is dated from around 300 to 500 CE.

To write this book, I followed this routine: Each morning, after a light breakfast, I would retreat to my study and perform the brief ritual that Goodman and Gore have developed to initiate ecstatic trance. In this ritual, after smudging and calling the spirits of each direction, I stand with my hands on my lower abdomen, feeling it rise and fall with each breath. This breathing from my diaphram brings my attention to my center of harmony, a focus of attention that I then carry with me as the drumming starts and I stand, sit, or lay in the selected ecstatic posture. This center of harmony is that place where I hold my hands, just an inch or two below my umbilicus. From my experience with Tai Chi I find that focusing on my breathing from my diaphragm t'ai chi brings me into a deep state of harmony. This state of harmony is one where deer, rabbits, and birds have physically approached me, a state that does not communicate a threat to other animals. In this ritual I then sit in the Freyr Diviner posture, pictured on the cover of *Baldr's Magic,* and I generally ask the simple question, "What's next?"

---

*These books represent the teachings referred to as the Cuyamungue Method, which represents the original research and findings of Dr. Felicitas Goodman. Dr. Goodman's work focused on the use of ancient sacred practices and postures that, when properly used, provide an experience that creates a doorway to an ecstatic experience of expanded reality. To learn more about Dr. Goodman's original work in ecstatic trance and her development and use of the Cuyamungue Method, visit the Cuyamungue Institute's website, www.cuyamungueinstitute.com.

The Freyr Diviner Posture

Sit cross-legged with the right leg in front of the left. Your left hand clasps the ankle of your right leg, while your right hand clasps or strokes your chin or beard. Your right elbow rests on your right knee if your beard is long enough; otherwise, place your elbow above your knee. Look straight ahead with eyes closed.

The experiences I would have in this posture were from the perspective or through the eyes of Queen Wealhtheow, or any of the three shamans I mentioned earlier: Vanadisdottir, Forsetason, or Healfdall. I began this book with questions as to how women who give birth, who naturally nurture and have compassion for others, and who in antiquity worshipped the Great Mother could relate to and deal with the emerging culture of men who value physical strength and aggression. I sought answers to my questions through Queen Wealhtheow, whose name was in these experiences from the beginning. Otherwise the names of the three shamans were not part of my initial experiences until I gave them their names, but I found myself very much one with these four people, seeing what they saw and journeying as they journeyed. I cannot say that the experience is of the actual historic activities of these figures, but I experienced them as land spirits of places I have visited in Sweden and Denmark, spirits that have something important to teach. In the same way that nighttime dreams are metaphoric experiences of life's activities, these ecstatic experiences are metaphoric descriptions of the activities of the characters of the story. To offer an example of a metaphoric creation in ecstatic trance, I once saw a large orange moon, while the person standing across from me in our ecstatic trance group saw a large wheel of orange cheese. The experiences were clearly related or connected, yet different. Being able to read each other's mind in this way is an example of connecting with the Universal Mind.

As the days went by I never considered what would happen next except for the knowledge I had of the epic poem *Beowulf,* which was alive inside of me, and so the story flowed from one ecstatic experience to the next. In this way I felt that the book wrote itself. The story takes place primarily in two locations: in Scania, which is the southern tip of present-day Sweden, at Trelleborg; and at Hleidargard, which is now Gammel Lejre, in present-day Denmark. I have been to both places twice, in 2004 and again in 2006, and have a good visual picture of what both are like today. In 2004 I actually walked about six miles exploring the area in and around Gammel Lejre and the nearby

Historical-Archaeological Research Center. Both places felt very spiritual to me. The moors and fens of Gammel Lejre are real, and I have walked them. I sat in the center of the remains of what is believed to be Heorot, the great hall of Hrothgar. I also walked the reconstructed site of the archeological remains of the medieval fortification at Trelleborg, a fortification built much after the time of Olaf, Wealhtheow's father.

The settlement of this ancient king was protected by the water of an estuary that flowed in and around his hall. I have also driven from Heorot north, and down to the fjord that would be King Healfdene's harbor. I have also driven up and down both sides of the strait between Zealand and Sweden. What initially took me to Gammel Lejre was reading *Beowulf: An Introduction to the Study of the Poem,* by R. W. Chambers, a book about the legendary figure Beowulf that includes the author's research of this epic poem. The reason for my going to Trelleborg is that it is the home of my wife's ancestors. I am sure that these visits increased the vividness of my ecstatic experiences while writing this book.

Jean Gebser states, "The disruption of space by time does not lead to emptiness or nothingness, but to transparency."[2] I believe that my disruption of space and time through ecstatic trance has offered me this transparency of antiquity that is in no way empty—that indeed I have made a connection to the reality of the magic and myth of the people of ancient Denmark and Sweden. What I experienced in my ecstatic trance journeying now follows in these pages.

1

THE VISITING
MERCHANT

As described in the introduction, my methodology in writing this book involved a daily routine: Each morning I would retreat to my study and enter ecstatic trance, generally using the Freyr Diviner posture (although as you read on you'll find that certain other postures seemed more appropriate for addressing certain questions). In my visits with the Nordic god Freyr, I had many questions, which he readily answered. In my search for understanding how the nurturing women of the transitional era could deal with the violence of men, my first questions were about Queen Wealhtheow, consort of King Hrothgar. Who is she? Where does she come from? And what is her life like? Over a period of a week I asked these questions each morning while sitting in the Freyr Diviner posture. My visions, and her story, evolved before me.

The ecstatic experiences came in a flow of images that gave me much to describe and expand on in my writing. Each chapter took around a week to write and involved approximately seven ecstatic experiences, one per day. As the chapter progressed, the questions I asked the spirit of the Freyr Diviner would usually involve what happened next in the unfoldment of the story. I would pose my questions in this kind of very general way, but sometimes I would be more specific, depending on what was happening in the narrative. For example, in this chapter, after Wealhtheow sees the ship coming toward the harbor, I asked Freyr when the king's sentry would see the ship—a question that assumed that in such a settlement there would be a sentry on duty. Then when the merchant ship arrived, I asked about what the king and the people of the settlement do in greeting the merchant. So each morning I asked a question that would take the narrative a step further. In this way the book took me approximately twenty-eight weeks to write.

Thus, the story begins . . .

"Your work is beautiful. Your threads are pulled evenly, as good as most grown-ups." The priestess Vanadisdottir was looking over Princess Wealhtheow's shoulder as she worked on her tapestry.

The princess was sitting with her loom on the knoll outside her father's great hall. Below her were the waters of the estuary that encircled much of the low knoll. The water breathed slowly with the tides of the great sea that lay before her. Her weaving was of a ship lined with men at the oars. She was imagining this ship coming up to the great hall. She looked up at Vanadisdottir with a dreamy smile. The princess's guvernante, her teacher and governess, knew what the girl was thinking—that someday she would meet some powerful prince to wed.

Princess Wealhtheow was the daughter of Olaf, king of the land of Scania, known much later as Skåne, Sweden. The hill she sat on would someday be called Trelleborg, and there would be a strong fortress built there. As it was, Olaf's large hall and the many surrounding buildings were well-protected by the estuarial waters of the sea and Olaf's large force of retainers.

Wealhtheow was only eleven years old, but Vanadisdottir, a priestess of the goddess Freyja, had been at her side since her birth and knew well her charge's mind. The princess had grown up watching the powerful warriors known as *berserkers* fighting, practicing on the same hill on which she now sat. She heard the shouts and cheers of onlookers watching the feats of strength of these men. She knew that her father, the king, valued this kind of strength, and that her mother, Gunheid, felt protected by it, but her mother also knew the teachings of the old ways and the healing and loving power of the Mother Goddess Freyja. For this reason the young woman saw no purpose in such fighting. That is just why Gunheid had chosen Vanadisdottir to care for and teach Wealhtheow— she did not want her daughter to forget the old ways of Freyja.

"Here comes a ship now!"

"What? How do you know? I can't see one." Wealhtheow was looking in the direction of Vanadisdottir's gaze.

"It's time I teach you how to see. Take a deep breath. Let it out slowly and move your attention to your belly, just below your umbilicus. Feel yourself relax into that spot. It might help for you to stand and hold your hands over that spot, your center of harmony."*

Wealhtheow knew what her guvernante was doing. They had done this many times before. That spot was her center of harmony, her *hvilðgarðr*, and it felt good resting there. There the world becomes quiet and many unusual things happen. It was most fun to use that spot to get animals to come to her.

Once the princess was in her center of harmony, Vanadisdottir continued: "Let your eyelids droop. Let your eyes go out of focus and look out at the sea. Look to the horizon. Notice those translucent fibers of light glistening. Just watch them, follow them, and see where they take your eyes."

After a few moments a smile came over the princess's face. It was there. A ship just coming over the horizon from the west, from the goddess Gefjon's island, what many years into the future would be known as Zealand, but now the land of the King Healfdene. She always loved these visitors and the wonderful things they brought to trade.

Vanadisdottir continued, "Stay in your place of harmony while you watch."

Wealhtheow's face again relaxed.

---

*This posture has been named the Bear Spirit posture by Felicitas Goodman, but the same posture is seen in several figurines found in Denmark and Sweden. More on the Bear Spirit posture can be found in Goodman's *Where the Spirits Ride the Wind*, 100–108.

The Bear Spirit Posture

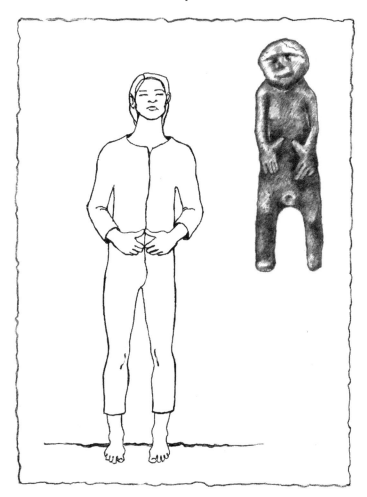

Stand with your feet parallel, about six inches apart, with toes pointed forward and knees not locked but slightly bent. Your hands are resting relaxed on your abdomen, with your thumbs touching and fingers spread apart and flat or together and bent under, such that the first knuckles of your index fingers are above your navel, forming a triangle. Your elbows rest easily at your sides. Your eyes are closed and your head is gently tipped back, as though you're looking at a point where the wall meets the ceiling.

"Notice the sentry standing over there scanning the horizon. He does not see the ship, and he won't for another hour or two. He tires his eyes looking and looking but not seeing. When I was trained in this way we lived in the woods, and we would use this way of seeing to find the many animals around us that even the greatest hunters among your father's retainers could not see. That you already know, and you have learned that the animals will come to you just as Odin's wolves came to Freyja. Now the merchant ship comes to you. Go back to your weaving. Maybe you can trade it for a gold brooch or something from some distant land."

The shadow cast by the princess's loom had doubled in length by the time the sentry turned to run toward the great hall with a shout that a ship was coming. Again Wealhtheow looked up at her teacher with a smile, and Vanadisdottir smiled back while doing her own needlework.

The people of the settlement came running down to the seaside to greet the approaching vessel. When the ship came ashore, the sailors jumped out, formed a line, and began passing the merchant's goods to dry ground. Others among the king's people were busy preparing a welcoming feast for the visitors. The princess and priestess sat off to one side watching the bustle of activity. Soon a tall man, richly dressed, strolled up the knoll. He was different from the others. His eyes were sharp. He seemed aware of everything around him. As he came to Wealhtheow he stopped to eye her work. With a gleam in his eye he said, "Princess, I'd like to see that when it's finished. I think you will be finished before I leave in a few days."

The sentry escorted the trader to Olaf's great hall and brought him before the king. Olaf greeted the merchant and offered him a seat next to his own high seat. He wanted to hear the news brought by this traveler. Wealhtheow snuck in and was sitting behind her father. She knew that he wouldn't mind as long as she remained quiet. He was proud of her curiosity.

The merchant related that he had been visiting King Healfdene, and he told Olaf of how this king's strength was growing. "He has many more retainers, and lesser kings and chieftains are paying him tribute for protection from the tribes to the south and the raiders." Olaf knew he would benefit by forming an alliance with Healfdene. He wanted to hear about Healfdene's sons, knowing that his daughter might be crucial in forming such an alliance. He would prefer to form this alliance through friendship and marriage rather than by flexing the strength of his retainers. Olaf is equal to Healfdene in his kingship—as evident in the amount of land he controls and protects, though he has considerably fewer retainers—but he is willing to show subservience to this powerful king from across the straits by accepting the title of chieftain in his presence in order to create this alliance of friendship.

"Healfdene's eldest son, Heorogar, has traveled far across the sea to East Anglia, where he is fostered with King Æðelstan. There he is learning to become a warrior, one of the best warriors in that distant land. Æðelstan loves him as his own son and hopes that he will stay to lead his retainers."

Wealhtheow loved the stories of distant lands. She dreamed of traveling the world to see these lands. She dreamed of being at Heorogar's side as he served in the court of King Æðelstan. Later, when the princess and her guvernante were preparing for bed, she excitedly told the priestess about Heorogar.

Vanadisdottir cautioned her: "I don't think he is the prince for you. I had a vision of you marrying his younger brother, Hrothgar."

"But why? Heorogar is in line to become king and I want to be his queen."

Vanadisdottir did not have an answer just yet.

The next morning the excitement in the settlement continued as the people traded for exotic things brought by the merchant. Word spread, and freemen or farming folk from the outlying areas traveled to the settlement. This day and the next were festive, with much food and drink. The drink, the essence of Kvasir, flowed freely. Occasionally a fight broke out because of too much mead, but that was rare and only added to the entertainment. The people would join in on one side or the other to cheer their champion.

When Wealhtheow inspected the merchant's goods her eyes fell on a silver pendant of a woman carrying a basket of apples. She recognized the design—the woman carrying apples was the goddess Idunn. She had heard and loved the stories of Idunn, stories of healing, not just with her golden apples—that story everyone knew—but stories told to her by Vanadisdottir of the goddess's use of other herbs and plants. The stories of Idunn's love for the god Bragi and his poetry were among her favorites.

Wealhtheow called to her father, "Papa, papa, look, look!" She excitedly showed him the pendant. He smiled and gave her a hug, but then returned to talking with the merchant. The merchant told of Healfdene's other sons. "Hrothgar, the second son, is at home and is becoming a respected warrior for his age. Halga, the youngest, just got his own sword."

Wealhtheow continued to eavesdrop and thus heard about the other princes. Meanwhile, Vanadisdottir saw that the pendant was of interest to Wealhtheow and recognized another opportunity to teach her about Idunn's powers.

"Look over there. That's something we need to collect—*martrem*. Feverfew is something we need with all the festivity and drinking going on. It is good for headaches, and by morning there will be many."

Vanadisdottir was respected by the community for her powers of healing, powers that Wealhtheow was learning too. Vanadisdottir was called to help whenever someone was injured or ill, and the princess was usually with her. But for now Wealhtheow knew she needed to return to her weaving, so she left Vanadisdottir to her plant collecting; she wanted her tapestry ready to trade for the pendant, and the priestess understood.

A day or two later, the merchant began packing his wares. His new acquisitions were already aboard the ship when Wealhtheow was finally finished with her weaving. She ran to him hoping that no one else had taken the pendant. She was pleased to find that he still had it. He had seen her looking at it and had saved it for her, knowing she wanted it. Both were pleased with the trade, though the trader extolled the value of the silver and made it sound as if, being a princess, she was taking advantage of him.

The merchant was about ready to push out to sea to head east along the coast, heading for one of the greatest trading centers of the north, Birka. From there he would head farther north and inland, to a lake where Wealhtheow's tapestry would be traded. Many years later it would be found near the Överhogdal church and hung in a nearby museum.

2
WEALHTHEOW'S BROTHER

As the lives of young Wealhtheow, her father, Olaf, and especially Wealhtheow's guvernante, the priestess Vanadisdottir, flow before me, I ask Freyr to show me more about the royal family. As the story unfolds, Olfdene, Wealhtheow's older brother, comes into the picture, and questions regarding what happens to him come forth, questions that I put to Freyr, questions that I ask each step of the way until I find out he is exiled to England. I also ask Freyr questions regarding Vanadisdottir's magical powers and her use of the ecstatic postures, and am provided fascinating answers . . .

Wealhtheow, at age eleven, had an older brother, Olfdene, who was thirteen. Though she loved Olfdene dearly and he was very protective of her, he also frightened her, beginning right after his twelfth birthday when their father gave him his first sword. The sword made the boy feel important, grown up. He constantly swung it, an act encouraged by his father, and his father showed him many of the finer techniques in swinging it. It became Olfdene's life, something expected of most boys in their journey to becoming men—that is, if they ever made it to adulthood.

One important person, Olfdene's best friend, didn't make it. He was twelve years old and had also gotten a sword for his birthday. He loved his sword every bit as much as Olfdene loved his own, and he was learning, too, how to swing it.

For Olfdene, next to his sword, his dog was most important. His dog was a very good rabbit hunter, so he had named it Rabbit. One day, when his friend was swinging his sword, he accidentally swung it at Olfdene's dog and cut off its head. In a fury Olfdene swung his sword and did the same thing to his friend. The loss of his friend changed Olfdene's life forever. He could no longer live at home in Scania; if he did, his head would likely be severed by his friend's father or brother in an act of revenge. And so Olfdene had to run and hide before his friend's father found out. He hid in a place where the underbrush was thick. He had thought of hiding in a cave that he and his friend had frequented, but he knew that it would be the first place others would look. The people in the settlement were pounding their chests in grief, as much for Olfdene, who would have become the next king of Scania, as for the death of his best friend. The king and queen went to the queen's hall and were not seen for several days, so desperate were they in their grief and in trying to figure out what to do. It was Vanadisdottir who could see, who knew where Olfdene was hiding. It was Vanadisdottir who took the boy food in the darkness of night.

In searching for what to do, Olaf could have banished the murdered boy's family and even the friends of this family, but this would not have been fair. What might have been most fair and kept the peace among the greatest number of people would have been to behead his own son, but he would have lost the affection of others, and besides, this idea was totally repugnant to Olaf. The only option was for him to banish Olfdene forever and hope that he had the wits to survive. To this end Olfdene had, in a sense, already banished himself; he knew that he was an outlaw to those whom he had once considered family and friends. The only contact he had with the settlement was through Vanadisdottir, and she kept the secret of her contact with the young prince, knowing that her life could be in jeopardy too.

Finally, Olaf made his decision and called for Vanadisdottir. He knew that if anybody knew where Olfdene was, it would be the priestess. A ship had come into the harbor, but no one had taken much interest in it because of the fear and grief that had overcome the settlement. The ship was on its way to England and had pulled into the harbor for the night because of inclement weather. Olaf knew of the Danish chieftain Æðelstan. Though he was called a king by those who live in his domain, as was Olaf, he was in the line of the Skjǫldung, and the Skjǫldung king was Healfdene. Olaf was king of Scania, the land across the straits from the lands of the Skjǫldung.

Olaf spoke to the captain and offered him a sum of gold if he would pick up Olfdene at a predetermined place farther up the coast of Scania. Vanadisdottir was to secretly take Olfdene to this place, with enough gold to pay for his passage to England. Olaf asked the captain to ask Æðelstan to look after the boy, even if it was in the capacity of a slave. He used the title *king* when speaking of Æðelstan because he knew it was to his advantage to show this respect to him. After all, he was the leader of the new Danish settlement in East Anglia,* though this settlement had not yet attained the status of kingdom. Thus Olfdene boarded the ship, his family not knowing if they would ever see him again.

When Vanadisdottir reported that she had accomplished her task, Wealhtheow and her mother, Gunheid, cried knowing that this boy had to leave home before he was ready. Their tears continued for days and became a concern to Vanadisdottir. The priestess was able to see into the future while lying on her seiðr bench. She retreated to this high platform to see what she could see. She knew that to go on a spirit journey she would need to lie on her stomach with her arms outstretched and her ankles crossed.†

---

*Modern-day England.

†This underworld posture is known as the Sami Lower World posture since it was found in the literature about the Sami reindeer herders of Finland. More on the Sami Lower World posture can be found in Gore's *Ecstatic Body Postures,* 186–90.

The Sami Lower World Posture

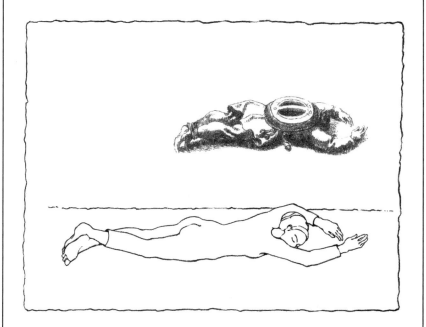

Lie on the floor on your stomach with your face down and arms extended above your head, your right arm extended a little farther than your left. Rest your cupped hands with fingers together face down on the floor about five inches apart. Extend your legs, with your right ankle crossed on top of your left ankle. Turn your head to the right.

In this position and from her center of harmony, her hvíldgarðr, Vanadisdottir began a journey that took her to England, to the battlefields of King Æðelstan. It was sometime in the future. There she saw Olfdene fighting valiantly in battle. When she returned from her seiðr journey she had a hopeful report for the king and queen. She told them that she saw Olfdene fighting under the banner of King Æðelstan and alongside Prince Heorogar, fighting the Angles to expand the Danes' territory. The ship carrying Olfdene had left Scania late in the season, a more dangerous time to travel, and yet Vanadisdottir's vision of Olfdene reassured the queen that her son would make the journey safely. The priestess couldn't tell the whole story just yet—that she saw both warriors fall in battle. But in Vanadisdottir's vision Olfdene was clearly a mature warrior. She told her charge, the princess, that her brother would become strong, though she did not know the outcome of his final battle—whether he would go to Valhalla, the upper-world realm where brave fallen warriors went, or to Gæfuleysabjarg, in the realm of Freyja. A warrior who died in his first battle went to Gæfuleysabjarg, the Cliff of Lucklessness, rather than Valhalla. From there, if the warrior remembered the ways of Freyja and the Great Mother, Moðir, his journey after death could take him to Griðbustaðr, the Dwelling Place of Peace. Most warriors had their eyes set only on Valhalla, the place of eternal battle. Vanadisdottir's hope, though, was that even these men would eventually find peace.

As Vanadisdottir and Wealhtheow sat together beside the fire in their hall of the queen, she told the princess about Griðbustaðr, the Dwelling Place of Peace.

"You know the stories of Valhalla, of warriors who die honorable deaths in battle, who go to Odin's Valhalla, where they continue to fight every day and if killed or injured come back to health to fight the next day. I also told you the story of how Idunn, with her healing apples and other herbs, brings the warriors back to health, and how no one had ever noticed much less thought of telling of her wandering through the fields of the dead and wounded. Another nearly forgotten story needs to be retold, the story of those warriors who die in their first battle. It is the preferred story, at least a story of greater hope, the story of the way it was before the destruction of Vanaheim, the upper world realm of the Vanir—a story that is still possible; the story I would hope for Olfdene.

"You may have heard that Freyja takes half of all those who die in battle. That is not totally true. She takes those who die in their first battle. She takes them to her realm, where they sit across the Gorge of Sorrow, Harmagil, across from the maidens who died as virgins. These maidens are claimed by the goddess Gefjon and reside in her Weeping Fields, Gratajöð. There they can see one another across Harmagil and spend their time grieving their shame. The hope is that they will eventually remember the ways of the Vanir and know that by using the power of seiðr they can cross the gorge and find their way to Griðbustaðr, where they can find peace and contentment.

"The warrior who dies in his first battle may reject the magical ways of Moðir or may have forgotten or never learned of these ways of the Great Mother. Hopefully, Olfdene will remember these ways, as I have taught both him and you."

These stories took Wealhtheow out of her pain, at least for the time being. They were stories of hope, stories that showed her that life could be different, better than living by the sword.

3

THE VISIT
FROM HEALFDENE

We have heard of King Healfdene and his oldest son, Heorogar, the prince of Wealhtheow's dreams. My questions now revolve around this king, his son, the prince, and the belief that the princess's dreams will not be fulfilled. The answers provided by the spirit of Freyr are found in the story of King Healfdene's visit to Scania.

One day the following spring, while Wealhtheow and Vanadisdottir were visiting a family that lived a short distance from Olaf's hall, they heard a blast from the horn of the sentry announcing an approaching ship. The priestess could not leave because she was delivering a baby. Wealhtheow was standing in the doorway, drumming for this soon to be mother, and looking back and forth between the woman in child-birth and the ship coming into the harbor. It was large and fancy, the ship of a king. She recognized the banners as those of King Healfdene. She was pulled two ways. She knew that her drumming for the priestess and the mother was crucial, and that the incoming ship would still be there after the baby was born.

Wealhtheow knew that poems have great power, the magical pow-ers of Bragi, the god of poetry. He was very skilled with words, words that rhymed and were spoken with a beat. It was Bragi who made the words magical, giving them their power in song. To emphasize the rhythm of the poem he made a drum and would recite his poetry to the beat of the drum. He saw how the sound of the drum would reverberate through the listener's body and block other thoughts and sounds, allowing the poem to enter the person with great purity. Thus Bragi brought us the drum. These drums were made in many ways, sometimes of wood and sometimes of pottery, most often with the hide of a sheep, but sometimes with the hide of other animals. Bragi's drum was made from the hide of the auroch, the ancestor of today's domestic cow. When Vanadisdottir was in training to become a priestess of Freyja she made her drum, which was very special because the sheep's hide she used was soaked in the sacred pool of Freyja. Vanadisdottir had made Wealhtheow's drum from a sheep hide soaked in the pond near the sauna where they often bathed, because it had become sacred to her, too.

Vanadisdottir had a number of poems she used on different occasions, but the one she sang most often, "Plants of the Mother," was very simple, and it was the one she used today.

Listen to the plants *Listen to the Mother*
The plants of the Mother *Make us well*
Listen to the plants *Listen to the Mother*
Use these plants *To keep us well*

Vanadisdottir would recite this poem as she prepared the plants she collected for someone she was caring for, and as the person would drink or eat the preparation she would recite this simple poem to the beat of her drum. When Wealhtheow made rounds with Vanadisdottir she would carry her drum and beat it along with Vanadisdottir. If Vanadisdottir's hands were busy, as they were today in helping this woman in labor, Wealhtheow would do the drumming alone for her.

Wealhtheow knew that a princess should be present in the formal greeting of a king, and the ship that was now in the harbor was that of a king. When she heard the cry of the baby she ran over to see the newborn. It would be no more than a few minutes before she would be free to go fulfill her duties as a princess. Vanadisdottir soon had the baby cleaned and wrapped. She handed the little girl to Wealhtheow, who held it for a few moments before laying it in the arms of the mother as she asked permission to leave, leaving the priestess to finish her work in caring for and instructing the new mother.

Wealhtheow hurried down to the estuary to stand at her father's side to greet the king. It was just as she had suspected: King Healfdene from across the strait, the father-in-law of her dreams. She knew she had to stand quietly, with a stately presence, though in her excitement she wanted to blurt out her excitement. Healfdene and Olaf embraced. In front of King Healfdene, Olaf took the position of high chief, a high-ranking, favored chieftain. He knew that the way to gain Healfdene's affection was to be deferential and accepted his title with grace. After a few words that Wealhtheow did not hear because of her excitement, her father put a hand on her shoulder and she heard him introducing her to the king. She held out her hand, and her dreamed-of future father-in-law gently took her hand to his lips. While they stood there she did not dare take her eyes off him, but from the corner of her eye she was searching around hoping to see a young man dressed as a prince. Wealhtheow then heard her father ask Healfdene about his sons. The response was that from all reports his oldest son was making a good name for himself in East Anglia, though the king had not seen him in four winters. Heorogar was his hope for the future. His younger sons were not mentioned.

They soon made their way to Olaf's hall, where feasting and drinking commenced, a celebration that would last into the evening. Olaf's men knew to make room for Healfdene's men in the great hall. Some of those of Olaf's men of lesser status stayed in outbuildings, likely with their women. A few of the more respected retainers mingled with Healfdene's men and found places in the king's hall to bed down later that night.

The high chief and king had their heads together talking for much of the night. Only late the next day did Wealhtheow learn the purpose of the king's visit and what they had been talking about. Wealhtheow's mother called for her from her private abode: the king was seeking a wife for his oldest son, she said; after all, it was spring. The girl's heart leaped—her dream was coming true!

Healfdene had two important reasons to make this marriage: one was to strengthen the bond with Olaf and between their two realms; the other was to bring his son, the crown prince, closer to home. He would not live forever, and when his son became king it would be over all of Denmark. The realm of the Skjǫldung would then stretch across Jutland, Zealand, and Scania, and with the new settlement in East Anglia it could stretch even farther. Denmark would become the powerhouse of the north. It would have control of all the seas, from the west to the lands of the Ynglings, what many years later would be known as Gammel Uppsala, Sweden. In this way Healfdene would control all trade. He also dreamed of eventually bringing peace to the north. It was the raiders from the sea who hampered safe trade. If he could stop their passage through the various straits of Denmark, peace and security in Denmark would be established for future generations.

Olaf's thought behind the marriage between his daughter and the son of the king was that he would then become part of the Skjǫldung dynasty, and his grandsons could become the greatest of kings. Hil! to Odin, the wisest of the gods!

When Wealhtheow related all this to Vanadisdottir, the priestess gasped.

Wealhtheow asked, "What's wrong?"

Vanadisdottir hesitantly answered, "I do not see . . . I do not predict this marriage. In my vision it is his younger brother, Hrothgar, I see you marrying."

Gunheid's hall, though smaller than Olaf's great hall, like her husband's was constructed of large wooden beams cut from the trunks of pines, supporting a roof of thatch. Occupying the center of the hall was a rock hearth for a fire, with smoke holes at either end in the eves that gave the only light in the hall. The smoke rose from the fire to exit through these openings. The dim light was such that Gunheid couldn't see the tears and redness in Wealhtheow's face when she entered her mother's hall. Her mother was lounging on the bench alongside the wall when Wealhtheow came in and sat down beside her. It was then that her mother could sense her daughter's grief.

Gunheid held Wealhtheow away to look into her face as the girl sobbed, "I'm not going to marry Heorogar . . . Vanny told me I'm not going to marry him, but rather Hrothgar instead. That is what she sees."

All her mother could do was hold her daughter. There was nothing that could be said.

Word of the priestess's vision quickly got back to Olaf, and he called for Vanadisdottir. She told him what she had seen on her seiðr journey, and he asked her if she could learn more.

"I think I could receive a deeper and clearer picture at the sacred pool of Freyja. The energy of that spot is where I learned the ways of Freyja, and that spot can give me the clearest visions of the future."

"I will give you twelve of my best retainers to protect you on your journey to your sacred place to make sure you get back safely."

The priestess demurred, "But I can travel more safely and faster by myself."

"I can't let you go by yourself."

Vanadisdottir left saying, "I'll prepare to go."

Soon an old, dirty hag, bent over and dressed in rags, found Olaf outside his hall as he instructed one of his men about the trip. She pulled at the hem of his tunic, but he ignored her. She persisted, and finally he turned to her with a scowl of annoyance.

"What do you want, old woman?"

"I'm ready to leave."

He turned to continue his conversation with his retainer, not hearing her.

Again she said, "I'm ready to leave."

He looked at her, perplexed.

"I'm ready to journey to the pool of Freyja."

A slow smile came over his face. He could not at first believe what he saw, but then, knowing Vanadisdottir's peculiar ways, knew it was the priestess.

"I go by myself," and she quickly scooted off.

The king knew that neither he nor his men could follow her or find her; he knew of her ability to become invisible. Yet he sent his men out to patrol the way he believed she would go.

The following day King Healfdene prepared to leave for his return trip. He expressed appreciation and joy in the proposed marriage of his first-born son to Wealhtheow. Nothing was said about Vanadisdottir's vision. Gifts were exchanged, and after embracing Olaf in anticipation of becoming one family, the king and his entourage pushed off to sea. Upon reaching his home, Healfdene would be readying himself for another journey, a long one—to East Anglia, to bring home his eldest son and heir.

4

VANADISDOTTIR'S JOURNEY TO FREYJA'S POOL

We are learning about the magic of Vanadisdottir. She is about to travel to the sacred pool of the beautiful goddess Freyja, goddess of fertility and love, where she was first trained to be a priestess of Freyja. Olaf considers this journey dangerous. As I sit in the Freyr Diviner posture, I ask his spirit to tell me about this journey over the course of the next week, in particular about the magical ways by which she ensures her safety while traveling through dangerous outlaw country. When she finally arrives at the sacred pool I ask questions about what life is like at this special place, and in this I feel that by using a different posture, the Freyja Initiation posture (see page 96), a death-rebirth posture, I will gain more insight into her experiences at Freyja's sacred pool . . .

After bidding Olaf good-bye, Vanadisdottir first went to the chieftain's herd of horses, and as she stood by the fence she moved her attention to her center of harmony. She knew that the first horse that came to her while she did this would be the horse she would want for this journey, as it would be the horse that would best know her needs. One came to her. She named it Fyrstr, "First."

It was still fairly early in the day when Vanadisdottir departed, and by evening she was already near the edge of Olaf's realm. She was somewhat familiar with this country because she had once aided a farmer and his family who lived here. This family was sometimes raided by outlaws, and on one occasion the farmer's only son intercepted such a raid. When the boy attempted to chase them off, the outlaw had swung his sword at the boy, severing his ear and blinding him in one eye. The farmer had called on Vanadisdottir, and she had traveled there as quickly as possible. When she arrived, the boy was unconscious and had lost a lot of blood, but she had been able to save his life, and now he could do his share of the work on the farm. As a result, the family was greatly indebted to Vanadisdottir and welcomed her when she arrived to spend the night. They were excited to hear news of the world beyond their farm. Because of this incident, the outlaws now knew that this farm was protected by the chieftain, and so they generally kept their distance, yet the son was no longer as courageous as he had once been in facing the outlaws alone, should they come again.

Early the next morning the priestess resumed her journey, making her way to the border and into the land of outlawry. One punishment given by Olaf to men who have committed crimes is banishment, such that they must become outlaws. These outlaws were the terror of travelers. Vanadisdottir knew how to travel silently, and with her sensitivity to everything going on around her she had confidence in her ability to hear and see any outlaws before they could hear or see her. She rode for most of the day before she sensed danger. She quickly dismounted and shifted into her disguise of a cackling old hag. First she bedded her horse, Frystr, in a thicket and instructed the animal as only she could to lie still and remain quiet until he heard her whistle. She then put some distance between herself and the horse.

As she sat alongside the trail to wait, three men in tattered clothing came out of the woods. Vanadisdottir, as an old hag, held out her hands in a begging gesture. They asked her if she had seen someone on horseback. She cackled incoherently but waved her arm in the direction opposite her horse, and they quickly left in that direction. They were on foot, but in the woods a horse could move no faster. She returned to Fyrstr and lay down with him. She fell asleep knowing that he would let her know if someone was coming. After the sun went down, she arose to continue her journey on horseback. With her ability to see, and with the trust between her and the horse, they could travel better at night than during the day, as this would allow them to ride through open meadows and bypass the deep woods where the outlaws held out.

The next evening they came to a farmstead, and once again her ability to heal endeared her to the family. The farmer, she discovered, had been boar hunting and had been gored on the leg. Though no bones were broken he had gotten a nasty wound from the encounter. The priestess was invited into the farmer's home, where she dressed his leg with a compress of *kulsukker,* comfrey, and *hjulkrone,* borage. Both plants were easily found in the farmer's pasture. Vanadisdottir spent the night, and by morning he was resting quietly. She instructed his wife on how to clean the wound and change the dressing and departed, accompanied by the farmer's son, who rode with her to the border to ensure that her journey would be safe.

Then began the last leg of her journey. Being now in the domain of a king who supported the *helgatjörn,* or sacred pool that belonged to Freyja and the priestesses who resided there, she felt more secure, yet her ability to see and hear was what really kept her safe. Riding in the open, she soon met a warrior of the king. After Vanadisdottir identified herself, he escorted her to meet the king. Such travelers were appreciated because of the news of distant lands they carried. After an audience with the king and queen, she was soon on her way to her final destination.

It felt good to be home. She quickly learned the sorrowful news that the high priestess who had trained her had died. But she loved the new high priestess, whom she had known from the time of their early training together. One of the novices showed her to the small hut for visiting priestesses. Vanadisdottir ducked under the door into its shelter of thatch. She carried nothing with her except her shawl and ever-present medicine bundle of herbs and potions. She set these items down on her mat of straw. Already on her mat was a robe worn by the priestesses. She changed into this robe before leaving the hut to tend to Fyrstr. After such a journey she felt a close bond with the horse and so wanted to show her appreciation by brushing and combing him well, using an antler comb.

Vanadisdottir easily fell into the routine of the other priestesses and novices. The next morning at sunrise she quietly left on her own to walk in the woods, picking berries, nuts, and other plants. For their first meal all of the priestesses and novices quietly and singly walked their own individual paths collecting their morning meal, gathering enough but no more than needed for this simple meal. Only after they returned and all that they had gathered was placed on a table did they start to talk quietly, praising Freyja and the other goddesses, especially Idunn, for their morning meal, while busying themselves preparing the food.

It was during this time that Vanadisdottir told the high priestess the reason for her journey. As expected, nothing was said, but the high priestess praised Freyja with a smile. Vanadisdottir knew the meaning of that smile—that she was to use her skills of seiðr as taught by Freyja. She knew each of the methods of seiðr: she could travel on a spirit journey to see into the future to ask the goddess a question. Or she could journey to the underworld, or go within herself or another person for the purpose of healing. She knew the postures for each type of seiðr. But on this journey her intent would be to look into the future. The way of seiðr in this sacred place was to squat on the mound or vulva of Freyja, the mound surrounding the dark pool of water, the helgatjörn. There, looking deeply into the dark water, she could see into the future. The helgatjörn was every bit as powerful—possibly more powerful—than sitting on the high seiðr platform, or *seiðhjallr,* that she normally used at home in Scania. It was on a high branch in a tree that Freyja herself had learned these powers.

To prepare herself for the helgatjörn, Vanadisdottir had to first cleanse herself in the sauna, something she was looking forward to after her long journey to this sacred place. After breakfast, she walked down the path to the *bastu,* the sauna hunt, which sat above the shallow ravine where the sacred tarn was located. The path was cool and damp. Soft moss grew along its sides. She arrived, disrobed, hung her clothing on a nearby tree, and then entered the bastu. For a moment the heat took her breath away. She sighed, letting any tension flow out of her body as she moved her attention to her hvilðgarðr, her center of harmony. As her eyes adjusted to the darkness she realized someone else was in there with her—her dear friend, the high priestess. They talked quietly of Freyja, and as they did the high priestess asked Vanadisdottir if she would teach the novices the eight journeys of seiðr. After all, she was recognized by the community as one of the best in such journeying. She was honored by this request and told the high priestess she would begin the next morning.

Next to the sauna was another small tarn in which the women would dunk themselves to cool down after sitting in the sauna. After entering the sauna three times and cooling down after each round, Vanadisdottir completed the cleansing ritual and was ready to sit on the vulva of Freyja. She left the hut to find that her clothing was gone and in its place a fresh linen robe with a hood hung. She put it on and continued down the moss-lined path to the sacred pool. Sitting on the mound beside the pool with her legs bent under her, lightly holding her thighs, she again went into her center of harmony while looking into the dark water of the sacred pool.

She sat there for some time before a vision appeared in the depths of the water, a vision of Olfdene and Heorogar sitting together under a tree. Though neither knew that they were in line for becoming brothers through marriage, it was evident that they felt a bond. Heorogar was instructing Olfdene on how he should enter his first battle. Olfdene was excited about this milestone and felt very ready to face it. The vision then faded, and the next vision that came to her was the same one that she had seen earlier in Scania—the two warriors fighting under the banner of Æðelstan, and both of them falling under the ax of an Anglia warrior. The valley in which they fought was abloom with wildflowers, so she could tell it was autumn. Vanadisdottir felt the pain of their death and awakened from her trance sobbing and in a sweat.

She then returned to the quiet of her hut, for such journeys exhausted her and she needed a short rest before she could again join the others in their preparation of the noon meal. When she came out of her hut she found them walking back from their garden carrying several large squashes.

In the afternoon she joined the other priestesses as they sat in pairs in the woods. She sat with an eleven-year-old girl, Gudrid, who was new to the community. They each sat quietly with their attention on their center of harmony, looking into the woods. Vanadisdottir saw the rabbit before the novice did but said nothing as the rabbit hopped toward them, stopped, and just looked up and then back and forth between their two faces. A smile came over the novice's face, and the rabbit darted away when she lost her concentration. Vanadisdottir smiled and told her that she did well, and that holding one's attention on the center of harmony takes practice.

The next morning after their simple breakfast Vanadisdottir sat at the edge of the helgatjörn with five novices, explaining to them the eight kinds of journeys.

"When beside the helgatjörn or lying on a seiðhjallr, there are eight kinds of journeys you can go on.* Different postures lead to different experiences. To learn each kind of seiðr takes a lot of practice. The more you practice, the more control you will have over where and how you journey. Let's try one posture. Lie on your back with your feet toward Freyja's pool. This is a very powerful place. Let your left

---

*Here Vanadisdottir is referring to the eight types of journeys in Gore's *Ecstatic Body Postures,* 218–23.

arm rest comfortably at your side, with your right arm extended and relaxed above your head.*

"Close your eyes, move your attention to your hvilðgarðr, your center of harmony, and notice it rising and falling with each breath." The priestess then started drumming with a stick on a nearby hollow log. Such logs were found in various places around this sacred place for just this purpose. She watched the novices and paced her drumming to their breathing. Soon all five young women were breathing in unison to the beat of the drum. She then began to slow the beat down to slow down their breathing. Nothing was said for about twenty minutes while she continued to beat out a slow rhythm. She could see that all five young women were in a deep trance. If they had not gone into a trance, she would have started to beat the drum rapidly again in order to distract them from their thinking, since thoughts limit the depth of a trance. Each novice had already learned how to quiet the mind. When the drumming stopped, the novices slowly opened their eyes. Vanadisdottir then asked each of them to relate their experience.

The first to speak, Gudrid, the same novice whom Vanadisdottir sat with yesterday, reported that she felt herself slide down the slope and go feet first into the pool of water. She remembered being surprised because the water was warm. As she continued down into the water she found she could easily breathe underwater. It was so peaceful, and soon she came to a sleeping mat where she saw her mother, who had died a year ago before the novice was sent away to be trained as a priestess. She sat beside her mother and they talked quietly. Her mother was pleased about her daughter becoming a priestess of Freyja.

Vanadisdottir commented, "You miss your mother and wish for her approval."

---

*The posture being described by Vanadisdottir was found among the petroglyphs of Tanum, Sweden, thus it has been labeled the Tanum Sky World posture, though it is identical to the posture found by Felicitas Goodman, who named it the Osiris Upper World posture. In this case, because the banks of the pool are tilted at about 37 degrees, they provide the angle necessary for lying in this posture. More on this posture can be found in Gore's *Where the Spirits Ride the Wind,* 59.

The Tanum Sky World Posture

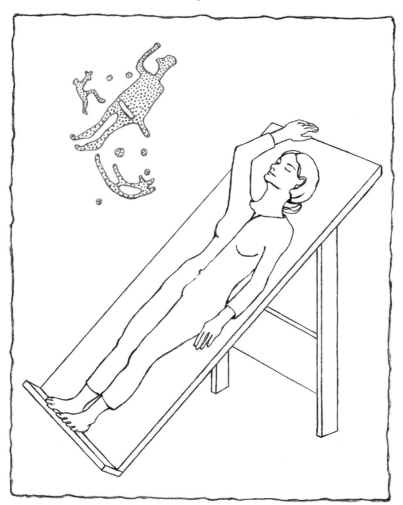

Lie on a launching pad*, a platform slanted at 37 degrees, strong enough to support a reclining person. Your legs and feet are together, your arms resting at your sides, or alternatively one arm—your right—or both may be raised above your head.

---

*The launching pad is a platform slanted at 37 degrees, strong enough to support a reclining person.

The second novice, Astrid, also went into the pool of water in her journey but dove in with her arms outstretched. She went to the bottom, and though the water in the pool was black, in her journey a light shined into the pool and she could see clearly. She swam with the fish, moving her feet back and forth like a tail. She wondered if she might actually have a tail but did not take the time to look because she was more absorbed in where the fish were taking her. She found herself in a cave—actually, the cave became the large hall of a king, and she was sitting in the hall telling stories to the king's two daughters.

This journey reminded Vanadisdottir of herself, and she suggested that this experience was likely a vision of the novice's future.

The third novice, Tora, happened to be lying with the heels of her feet resting on a rock at the water's edge. In her vision she felt herself push off this rock and soar into the sky. Using her wings, she soared and glided through the sky to land on a branch high in a tree. From there she could see the whole world below her. She could see the other priestesses and older novices working in the garden. She could see herself and the other four novices with Vanadisdottir lying beside the tarn. She then saw a boar digging with its snout in the woods not far from the garden. She felt a panic flow through her and wanted to shout a warning to those working in the garden. Then the boar turned and moved deeper into the woods.

After hearing the girl's vision, Vanadisdottir suggested that she needed to pay attention to or watch for a passing danger and realize that though she may feel threatened, the danger would pass.

The fourth girl, Inga, had a simple vision of being at home, sitting and watching the boys and young men fighting with their swords. Vanadisdottir asked her about her feelings in this vision, and she reported that she had no feelings but was just watching. As she thought about it, the girl was neither excited nor disgusted by their fighting.

Vanadisdottir reached out and held Inga's hand and with a smile said, "That is good. You see what men do. It may seem foolish, but you don't feel disgusted. Neither does it excite you. You just rise above it and let those followers of Thor do what they must."

The last novice, Asgerd, said that when she lay down beside the pool she was thinking about her sister who was about to get married. She was concerned about the man her sister was to marry. He was the son of a freeman, a farmer. The novice wanted something more for her sister. On her spirit journey she flew like a bird and found herself at a farm cut in the woods. It was a warm, sunny day, and she saw her sister spinning wool, looking very peaceful, while her husband, the farmer's son, was out cutting wood to enlarge the farm fields. With that vision Asgerd said she too felt very peaceful and was able to let go of her concern for her sister.

Vanadisdottir smiled and reached out and took the girl's hand, and said nothing for a few moments. Then she said, "That posture is one of several postures to use to go on a spirit journey. If you enter the journey with a question or concern, the journey may lead you to an answer. Sometimes it doesn't, and then you learn that you asked the wrong question or held an unimportant concern. You can make such journeys from a seiðr platform or beside a tarn. At this place of power journeying is easy. With practice you will find that other places are also easy. Other postures can take you on a journey within yourself, or others can be used for the purpose of healing, for visiting those who have died, and for looking beyond this life, for shape-shifting, and for celebration.

"What you did this morning showed all of you what can happen. One of you visited someone who died; several of you also shape-shifted and experienced personal healing on your spirit journey. On my journey here to this sacred place I used shape-shifting to travel safely. You have a lot to learn in your training as priestesses, and these journeys are but a small part of it. Other forms of seiðr are found in the power of singing—Hil! to Bragi—and the use of herbs—Hil! to Idunn. Each of you will find some power that is special to you. I wish you well in your training. Hil! to Freyja."

Each novice would receive a new name related to the name of Freyja after their second year of training.

That evening, Vanadisdottir ate her meal with the high priestess. Again they talked quietly, and Vanadisdottir told her that she would be leaving the next morning to return to Scania, and to her work there.

5

VANADISDOTTIR'S RETURN JOURNEY

As we will see, the revealed answers to my questions during her journey home are exciting and again of considerable magic, magic that she teaches to others. On this journey we meet the young son of the farmer who is disfigured, Thord, and the experience of him finding his stolen ram leads to more questions that are again answered while sitting in the Freyr Diviner posture. The resulting images show the extraordinary magical powers of Vanadisdottir, and now, Thord . . .

The next morning after breakfast Vanadisdottir mounted her horse and left. She rode for the day without any problems. She knew the king's men were watching her and protecting her. On her walk that morning before breakfast she had collected *berberis,* barberry, for the juice from the berry; she also gathered *vejbred,* plantain, and *rejnfang,* tansy, to fight infection, along with *baldrian,* valerian root, for pain. She had ground these herbs into a paste that she now carried with her. She was concerned about the farmer she had seen earlier who had been gored by the boar. The biggest problem with this kind of wound was infection, and though she had cleaned the wound as best she could with the herbs available, kulsukker and hjulkrone, there was a real danger that it would still become infected, so on her return journey she was prepared.

That evening when she arrived at the farmstead she found the farmer in bed, delirious and with a high fever. The wound was inflamed and oozing. She placed a piece of wood between his teeth to bite on while she opened the wound to first clean it with hot water and a boiled kulsukker leaf. She then spread the paste she had made into the wound and prayed to Idunn that he would recover as she sang "Plants of the Mother" and beat the rhythm on the family's drum. She sang it the entire time she was ministering to him, but now she could use her hand to beat the drum. She had seen worse who had recovered. His wife swabbed his forehead with cool water throughout the night. By the next morning he was resting more comfortably and his fever had broken. The priestess stayed another day to clean the wound and change the dressing several more times. By the second morning he was up and limping around, and Vanadisdottir knew he would survive. She left after giving his wife the rest of the paste and instructions on how to care for the wound, all the while praising Idunn and singing quietly the song "Plants of the Mother."

The priestess came to the end of the land belonging to the local king and planned to ride all day and night and the next day on her journey through the land of outlaws. Her senses were acute and twice she sensed danger. Both times she hid in wooded thickets, once in the mouth of a cave against a cliff, and both times the outlaws passed by, knowing nothing of her presence.

While resting next to the cave, she felt power emanating from within calling to her to enter. In the cave, the womb of Moðir, the grandmother of Freyja, she felt the presence of the Great Mother. She sat back against the rock wall and was not surprised to find herself sitting in a wall cavity that comfortably fit her back. It was a place where she belonged. She knew there was a message for her. She automatically moved to her place of harmony, and a vision came to her of a spring. Next to the spring grew a *rönn* tree, a mountain ash fully fruited with red berries. A short distance away below the spring the water again went underground. A handsome ram was bellowing, its front right leg sunk deeply in the ground just below the spring. Vanadisdottir saw from this vision an opportunity to teach someone about the Great Mother and her granddaughter Freyja, but she did not know when or how. She had faith, though, that she would recognize the opportunity when it was before her. She thanked Moðir and left the cave to continue on her way.

On a third occasion she again sensed danger. She was in an open meadow and had no place to hide when she saw a spear land not far from her. It was then that she appreciated the swiftness of her horse, Fyrstr, who quickly outdistanced the outlaws, who were on foot. She disappeared into the woods, where she was most comfortable during the day.

By night she had crossed the border and was again in the realm of Olaf, looking forward to staying with the family she had helped a couple of years earlier, with whom she had stayed on her way north. They again welcomed her warmly, as she knew they would. She found Thord, the son who had lost his ear and eye to an outlaw's sword, pacing in anger and frustration. He had lost his prize ram and had just heard that another nearby farmer had lost a ram too. He felt powerless to go after the outlaws. The neighbor saw where his fence was broken and found many footprints. He had followed them but lost them in a field of rocks.

The priestess told Thord about her vision of the stuck ram, and he knew the exact place she described—beyond their pasture, not far from the edge of Olaf's realm. He was up and grabbed her by the arm—"Let's go. I'll show you."

They soon were at the top of a low knoll looking down the other side, where she recognized the scene from her vision, the spring and the rönn tree. The bellowing ram was there too, with its leg stuck in the mud. Before they went any farther the priestess exclaimed "Hil! Freyja." Her vision from the womb did not fail her. She grabbed Thord by the elbow and motioned for him to wait a moment, asking him, "What do you see?"

With a look of surprise he answered, "Well, the tree, the spring, and the ram."

She then reached out and put her hand over his abdomen, just below his umbilicus, pressing lightly. "Look again."

This action in some way changed his perception. With his eyes fluttering he exclaimed, "The air next to the spring is shimmering."

"Watch the shimmer. Feel the warmth of the shimmer, of heat rising from the earth. Look at the earth below the warmth. What do you see?"

"The remains of a campfire."

"Sit with your legs crossed, your right leg in front of your left leg. With your left hand, grasp your right ankle, and stroke your chin with your right hand as if you were stroking a beard. This posture Freyr used to see into the future.* Look at the shimmer. Let your eyes droop, relax your body, feel the warmth in your belly where I placed my hand. Look and see." After a few moments she again asked him, "What do you see?"

Thord's mouth was hanging open. "Just for a moment I saw three men running away, herding a ram, not my ram, another ram."

"Remember what just happened. Now go and free your ram."

Thord mounted his horse and rode to the spring with his hound, Heim, running at his side. Vanadisdottir watched from the knoll. Thord found a stick, a branch from the rönn tree to dig away the mud from around the ram's leg. He found that the animal's hoof was stuck between two rocks and used the stick to pry the rocks apart. The ram was free, its leg unbroken. Taking the ram back to the priestess, he had not forgotten what had just happened.

She motioned for him to sit down. "You were injured by an outlaw's sword. You lost your ear and your one eye, but that does not mean you cannot see. You will likely never be a warrior, but you can learn to see what warriors cannot see, just as you saw the outlaws running away with your neighbor's ram. They left here before your ram arrived. He probably came to this place because of the scent of the

---

*This is the Freyr Diviner posture found on page 5.

other ram, to protect his territory. Your ram is safe. But you saw the outlaws herding your neighbor's ram. You know how to see, a power much greater than the power of a warrior, for greater than the power that destroys is the power that sees. Truly seeing can show you other ways to live.

"You can see the outlaws. I can see their arrogance, their foolish arrogance that will cause them to lose what they thought they have gained. I can see you stalking them with the silence of a cat. I can see you finding an opportunity to retrieve your neighbor's ram. They are not far off. They are bickering among themselves as how to share the ram. They will not get far.

"Kneel as I showed you before, next to the spring. That posture can help you see into the future. A spring with a rönn tree is a place of power. Kneel as I have shown you, move your attention to your center of harmony, your hvílðgarðr, where I placed my hand, breathe into that place, and let your eyes see the vision of the outlaws. You have the power to see."

He returned to the spring and did what she told him to do. He saw them walking and arguing, hitting and tugging at the ram to move him in different directions. Two of them got into a fight, while the third left with the ram. Thord went in the direction of the outlaws, soon finding one of them dead along the trail and the second hobbling off injured. Thord followed the tracks of the ram in the soft earth and ahead of him he then saw the ram herded by the one man. Thord knew what to do. He had herded sheep, grew up with sheep, they were his life. He had learned to bleat like a ewe. His sheep would come to him when he bleated. He called to his own ram in this way, even though the ram was with Vanadisdottir, out of sight and at some distance. No one can be certain whether the ram heard Thord's bleat, or if it was Vanadisdottir who heard it and whacked the ram on its rear. Either way, the ram ran off, leaving the priestess's side, and soon found Thord. The bleat also got the attention of the neighbor's ram, and now it had the scent of the other ram, too. The outlaw in his attempt to herd the ram could not compete with Thord's bleating and the scent and snorting of another ram.

Vanadisdottir soon saw Thord and his hound, Heim, herding the two rams toward her. One outlaw would not chance facing one shepherd alone. He had left, going in the opposite direction. Expressions were sometimes lost in the scars of Thord's right eye and ear, but his broad grin could not be mistaken.

As they continued back toward the steading, Thord's hound joyfully herded the two rams as Vanadisdottir reflected on the gods. "Your parents named you after the god of war, Thor. Their dream for you was to become a warrior for the king. Your family is free, and you now wander the fields as a shepherd. You have the power to see. You saw the outlaws and knew what you had to do.

"Thor did not always see, unlike his father, Odin. That was his problem. He could not see the tricks played on him by the giant Utgard-Loki. When challenged by the giant to compete to see who could drink the most from the giant's drinking horn, Thor could not see that he was drinking from the ocean. When challenged to see who could lift the giant's cat off the floor, he could not see that he was lifting Jormungand, the sea serpent. When challenged to wrestle Elli, the giant old crone, he could not see that he was wrestling death itself. You have heard these stories before. Thor's growing anger made him more and more blind to the giant's illusions.

"Odin can see, though the best seer of them all is Freyja. She teaches the world, at least those who believe in her, to see the way others cannot. They can see distant places as you did, places out of sight of the eye. They can see into the future. They can see inside of themselves and others to find what is wrong, so they can heal. They can visit those who have died. They practice seiðr. Some of the best seers are men, *seiðrmaðr,* male practitioners of seiðr. Yet sometimes the men who worship Thor look down on the seiðrmaðr because instead of worshipping Thor they worship Freyja, and Freyr, who could also see. Those who worship Thor have foolishly forgotten the power of the magic of the past. Yet the wise men of our people have not forgotten. I showed you that you could see, because I see you becoming one of those wise men who can help his people."

Thord thus began to learn the ways of the goddess.

The next morning Vanadisdottir left the steading to return to the settlement of Olaf. Thord rode with her. Some distance to the south was the next farm, the steading of Thord's uncle and aunt, his mother's sister. Thord enjoyed visiting with his two cousins so he needed no encouragement to travel with the priestess on the first part of her journey back to Scania. As they approached the farm they could hear a ewe bleating as if in pain. Vanadisdottir was quick to dismount and run to the ewe. She threw her arms around the ewe, lying against the animal's back with her hands pressing on the ewe's belly. In that position she could feel the bloating of her belly, but the priestess also had a vision, a vision of the ewe. She asked Thord to hold the ewe in the same way, to move his attention to his center of harmony and tell her what he saw. She placed her hand on his shoulder while he did what she had asked.

A few moments later Thord asked his uncle, "Where is the old hay you took out of the shed?"

His uncle pointed to a small pile of hay not far away, just next to the shed.

"She was eating that old, last year's hay."

Now Vanadisdottir's vision made sense. That hay was moldy and had been thrown out to make room to store the new hay for this winter. She saw the ewe eating from a pile of old hay and, even though she did not understand the problem as Thord did, she knew the remedy. She boiled a tea with mint and thyme and offered the ewe a drink of the warm tea. She then beckoned for Thord to sit down.

"You did it again. You could see in your vision the problem, but to see you used a different posture. When you sat with your legs crossed, stroking your chin, you were able to see into the future and rescue the ram. The posture I showed you for holding the ewe is for healing.* You held the ewe with your hands on her belly. Stand with your body relaxed, with your knees slightly bent, with your hands resting on your belly, with your pointing fingers pointing at your navel. Let your other fingers point downward at an angle. Feel the warmth of your belly, the warmth of your hvilðgarðr, and let the vision come to you. It will be a vision of healing. Embrace your sheep or others that may be sick in that relaxed bear hug and you will see what you need to do.

"Hil! to Freyja. She taught us this way to heal. When Idunn was kidnapped by the giant Thiazi with the help of Loki, she was not there to give the gods and goddesses her golden apples, which prevented them from getting old. Without the apples they got old and wrinkled and started to tremble. Freyja did too, even though she was younger than many of the gods. She was with Njord, her father, and watching him age so quickly greatly disturbed her. It was then in her grief that she gave him the bear hug. In this embrace Freyja saw the giant Thiazi holding Idunn in his mountain hall in Jotunheim. She hurried to tell Odin, who called together the Æsir. You remember the story—how Loki then shape-shifted into a falcon and flew to Thiazi's hall. Finding the giant gone and Idunn locked in the hall, he changed her into a nut to carry her back to Asgard. Thiazi saw him flying away and shape-shifted to an eagle for the chase. The Æsir, seeing the falcon and eagle racing toward Asgard, built a large fire behind the wall. Loki made it inside the wall safely, but Thiazi flew into the fire, which killed him. It was Skadi, Thiazi's daughter, who then became Njord's wife, but that is another story.

"It is from this story that we learn the healing power of the Bear Spirit posture."

The priestess then pulled from her pouch an amber amulet of a golden boar, the powerful steed of Freyja, and gave it to Thord. "This is the way of Freyja's journeys. I will show you other ways of seiðr when

---

*This posture, the Bear Spirit, is illustrated on page 11.

we again meet next spring, when you bring your winter wool to market. I'll be there."

She then rode off toward the great hall of Olaf. She brought them the news that they had feared: Heorogar and Olfdene would fall in battle. Her vision suggested that their deaths would come later in the autumn.

6

THE AUTUMN TRIP
TO DENMARK

Upon Vanadisdottir's return to Scania, I ask what will happen next regarding her vision of the deaths of Olfdene and Heorogar. It becomes clear that a trip to visit King Healfdene is necessary. My questions concern ship travel, what life is generally like in Denmark, and the Danish royal family's response to hearing the priestess's vision. I put these to the spirit of Freyr while sitting in his posture, and take an ecstatic trance journey to the island of Zealand, the home of King Healfdene . . .

The people of Scania had a good fall harvest. Grains and other vegetables were stored, eel and other fish smoked, and meat dried. Spirits were high with such preparedness for the coming winter. One day not long after the harvest, when the sky was blue and the sea calm, Olaf decided to make the journey across the narrow straits to Denmark, to visit King Healfdene. He felt some responsibility to tell his friend and ally about Vanadisdottir's vision. He maintained a ship in a harbor just across the strait, from where he could see the island of this great king, about a day's journey west from his settlement. That morning he, Gunheid, Wealhtheow, and Vanadisdottir left on horseback to cross the land, accompanied by a sufficient number of men to man the ship moored in the harbor. When they arrived at the harbor the sky was still blue and the sea calm. They were quick to board the vessel with their horses and move out, the oarsmen smoothly cutting through the water.

Upon reaching the other side they unloaded their horses and found a good place to set up camp, for it was still another day or two's journey up the coast to the northern tip of the island of Zealand, and then south into the deep fjord that protected the hall of the king. The next morning they started up the coast. When they arrived at the southern tip of the fjord, the king's sentry patrolling that shoreline saw them coming, recognized their banner, and rode off the short distance to the next sentry to inform Healfdene's consort, Queen Sigrid, of the coming of royal visitors, since the king had already left on a journey to see his son in England.

The settlement of Hleidargard—which in the distant future would be known as Leire, Denmark—came alive in preparation to receive the visitors, preparations directed by Queen Sigrid herself. She first sent a welcoming delegation to meet this important chieftain and his family and to escort them to the great hall where they were informed that the king himself had left Hleidargard for England just days earlier. She had arranged for a feast for the guests. The good weather had held for Olaf and his family's arrival that afternoon, although Wealhtheow's stomach was churning—not because of the sea voyage, but because she was about to meet her future mother-in-law and Prince Hrothgar, though he still knew nothing about the marriage foretold in Vanadisdottir's vision.

Because Heorogar was the first-born and in line to become king, Vanadisdottir felt that it was her responsibility to tell the queen about her vision of his death in a battle with the Angles. She knew that sharing this information would not change the course of his fate. The death of a son was always real and ever-present in the mind of a mother whose son was a warrior. Trusting the priestess's vision Sigrid broke into sobs upon hearing about the vision, and the priestess sat with her in silence to offer her support. Sigrid knew that the priestess would not take lightly the burden of carrying such news. The queen asked her if she had told Wealhtheow the vision, and Vanadisdottir replied that she had. Though some did not believe in such visions, Wealhtheow and her mother, Gunheid, followers of Freyja, had no doubts about them. Though Healfdene was a follower of Thor and Sigrid a follower of Gefjon, being a woman Sigrid had learned the stories of Freyja and respected the priestess and her vision. Sigrid only wished that Healfdene was there with her to hear of the vision and offer her support.

Wealhtheow spent some time with Princess Signy, knowing that they would one day be sisters through marriage. A pavilion had been built outside the great hall that had a central firepit, beside which the young women could sit to do their spinning and weaving in the bright light of this cool autumn day. Signy was a year older than Wealhtheow, who by now was thirteen, and they enjoyed each other's company while spinning the wool shorn from the sheep during the past summer, an unending task for all women, who made the fabric used in clothing for everyone in the settlement. At this time Signy was pregnant and staying with her mother, since her husband, Jarl Sœvil, was away collecting tribute for his father-in-law. In the shelter of the pavilion the young women had a good view of the youths of the settlement and could watch Healfdene's retainers practicing their skills in fighting. Neither Wealhtheow nor Signy could take their eyes off Hrothgar as he sparred with the other men of the king's retinue. He was proving to be a strong warrior, respected by all. Wealhtheow realized that she could find satisfaction in marrying him.

The two young women had much to talk about. Wealhtheow learned that Signy knew very little about Freyja, and that the people of Denmark worshipped Thor, while the women worshipped Gefjon, for if it were not for Gefjon their island would not exist. This goddess, in a deal made with the king of Sweden, used her four giant oxen sons to plow and drag land from Sweden to form the island of Zealand. This land was taken from what would be known in the distant future as Lake Vänern. If you look at a map you will see that Zealand and the lake are almost identical in size and shape. Gefjon is the mother of the Skjǫldungs and the great-grandmother of Signy, she told Wealhtheow. Gefjon was especially important for young women before they were married because it was Gefjon who received women who died as virgins into her realm, the place called Grðfgratabjǫð, the Weeping Fields. There they spent their time peering over the Gorge of Sorrow, Harmagil, watching those warriors who died in their first battle and who were taken to dwell in the realm of Freyja called Gæfuleysabjarg, the Cliff of Lucklessness.

Wealhtheow learned that Signy knew very little about seiðr and thought such magic was witchcraft. When Wealhtheow heard her say the word *witchcraft* in such a negative way, she began to feel sick to her stomach. What could she say? She told Signy, "The warriors who die in their first battle and the women who die as virgins don't have to remain in those realms of the upper world if they remember the powers of seiðr. Using the powers of seiðr they can journey beyond, to Griðbustaðr, the dwelling place of peace, where they can live together." Signy did not know what to say to this. She liked the idea but didn't know if she could believe it. She could not imagine warriors wanting to live in peace and believed that they all would want to find their way to Valhalla, the war-riors' heaven.

As Wealhtheow sat there with Signy, a messenger came to her ask-ing that she come for an audience with Queen Sigrid. As Wealhtheow entered the queen's hall, Sigrid motioned for her to come sit beside her. The queen still had tears in her eyes. Wealhtheow knew that she had received the news of Vanadisdottir's vision. The priestess had told the queen of the princess's grief upon hearing this vision herself. The queen said to Wealhtheow, "You should not have to grieve the death of your warrior even before you have met him. Healfdene told me about how excited you were with the thought of marrying my son. Well, if Heorogar dies as envisioned by the priestess, I still want you as my daughter-in-law and you shall marry Hrothgar. I know Healfdene would want that."

A smile showed through her tears as she spoke. Wealhtheow just sat there in silence looking into the queen's face as the queen took her hand and held it softly. Finally, Wealhtheow said, "Thank you," as tears rolled down her cheeks, too.

That evening at the feast, the two princesses sat next to each other at the table of the queen in Healfdene's great hall. Olaf and Gunheid sat on the other side of their hostess, the queen. Hrothgar sat at the head of the table of warriors. Sigrid passed a horn of mead to toast the guests. It was then that she announced, "There will be a day when we all can say we are one family of Skjǫldung." It was that last word that made this statement special, moving the meaning from a figurative family to an actual one. Everyone in the hall understood that special meaning.

That night spaces were prepared in Signy's hall for both Wealhtheow and Vanadisdottir. Signy also had a guvernante, Fiona, who loved her dearly and who also slept in her charge's hall; she was the childless wife of a farmer who had died defending the king. She had lost her child in birth and had been called on to nurse Signy as an infant. It was Vanadisdottir's way to tell a story about Freyja or Idunn to Wealhtheow before she went to sleep. Tonight she chose a story for both princesses— the story of how Freyja learned spirit journeying.

"Freyja had long ago learned that by quieting her mind and moving her attention to her place of harmony, her hvilðgarðr, the spot just below her umbilicus, animals would come to her. She loved to watch animals from her hvilðgarðr because then they would do those things that most people never see. One day she climbed a tree and found a broad branch that would hold her as she lay back to watch the birds. She lay there watching a bird, or two birds, a mother and a father bird, build a nest. They went back and forth to the ground and other places to pick up twigs and blades of grass and carried these twigs and grasses back to the nest, making it larger and stronger—a nest in which the mother bird would lay her eggs. As she watched, Freyja had an experience of leaving her body and flying through the air like the birds. It was an exhilarating experience, and while flying she could see herself lying on the tree branch and she also could see into the nest the birds were building. She tried this several times and found that she could explore the world with her new power, and that she could travel faster when she rode in her chariot drawn by her cats—in fact, she could travel without being seen.

"Yet the tree branch was quite uncomfortable, so she had the idea of building a flat platform of boards, as high as the limb of a tree but much more comfortable. She would lie on this platform on her back with one arm stretched above her head and the other arm down alongside her, and then move her attention to her center of harmony. In this position she could leave her body and fly anywhere she wished. She named this way to travel *seiðr,* and she named the platform the *seiðhjallr.* It was from this platform that she journeyed to try to find her husband, Odr. And it is from my seiðhjallr that I have learned to travel and have visions of the future.

"When I was trained as a priestess, we had the sacred pond of Freyja, formed by the tears of Freyja as she hunted for her husband. We would lie down beside that tarn to go on such spirit journeys, but I find that a high platform works just about as well. Signy, it was from my platform that I could see your brother fighting so valiantly for King Æðelstan. He is a great hero. And Wealhtheow, I could see your brother, Olfdene, fighting alongside him."

It was with this story of the two brother heroes that the two princesses fell asleep.

The next day the young women continued their spinning and weaving under the outdoor pavilion, where they had a central fire to keep their fingers warm in order to do their work. For their enjoyment Vanadisdottir told them another story.

"Frigg, who became the goddess of spinning, was out walking with Idunn, exploring the countryside, when she found some fibers caught on a bush, the wool of a sheep. She pulled the fibers off the bush and placed them in her pocket. Later, when sitting in the sun on the hillside, she pulled out her comb to comb her hair and out with it came the sheep's wool, which had gotten caught in the comb. She mentioned to Idunn how this wool stuck to everything. While they sat there quietly talking, she pulled the twigs and other stuff out of the wool and then started combing the ball of fluff with her comb, which had been made for her by Ullr. The wool combed out light and fine. She put her comb away, and as the two goddesses continued talking she absentmindedly started twisting the wool as she sometimes did her own hair, the same way one of her daughters would sit and twist her hair, a habit passed down through the generations. When her attention came back to what she had been doing with her fingers, she had a long strand of wool that she found was quite strong when she pulled on it. The fibers of the wool had stuck together with the twisting.

"Frigg wore a long braid that came over her shoulder. She took this long strand of wool that Idunn named *yarn* and tied it around her braid to hold it together. When the other goddesses saw what she had done with her braid, they wanted yarn to do the same thing with their hair. Frigg went to the shepherd whose sheep grazed on the hill and asked him to collect some wool for her, and she then showed the other goddesses how to comb it and twist it into yarn. Soon all the goddesses of the Vanir had yarn tied into their hair at the ends of their braids. Some of the gods even started using yarn to tie their pulled-back hair to keep it out of their eyes. Thus Frigg became the goddess of spinning. After learning how to spin the wool into yarn, they eventually learned how to weave it into warm and strong fabrics from which they began making clothing. Until that time, everyone wore animal skins to keep themselves warm."

That same day the men went out on a hunt. The night before, in preparation for the hunt, Olaf and Healfdene's men had built a large fire around which they sat making plans for the hunt. They were joined by about fifteen additional men, bringing the group up to about fifty men; the number of men would have been larger but for those who had accompanied Healfdene on his journey to England. The men decided that they would surround one particular stand of trees where deer tracks were plentiful, and then move in to meet in the middle with the deer trapped inside their circle. This they had done many times before, but with the additional men they were eager to hunt in this larger tract of woodland. As they sat by the fire, the men drew in the sandy soil in front of them pictures of men encircling a small herd of deer. They drew figures representing themselves running their spears into the deers' flanks, just behind the ribs and into the heart. In doing this they could feel power swelling in their arms and legs. This ritual preparation gave them the strength to have a successful hunt.

In the wee hours of the morning, well before sunrise, the men left the settlement and quickly rode to the spot where they had planned to hunt. Quietly, they surrounded the woods and started to move in, making sufficient noise to move any deer ahead of them. The circle slowly grew smaller and closed in on the deer. It was sometime after dawn when the circle became small enough so that the men could see one another from across the circle, in which stood five panicked deer. The men were ready when the first deer charged to get out of the circle. Four of them were quick to close the gap, and two spears were deeply set, sticking out one on either side of the deer. The next deer charged, and then the next. Quickly the hunt ended, and four deer lay dead. The deer were gutted and poles were cut. The carcasses were tied to the poles and carried back to the horses. Excitement was high as they rode back to the settlement leading the four pack horses carrying the deer meat.

There was enough fresh meat for that evening's celebration, as well as some for the visitors to take on their journey home the next morning, and even some leftovers to dry on the fire. Signy gave Wealhtheow a beautiful piece of red-dyed linen that she had been weaving and had just finished. Wealhtheow had earlier given her a tapestry she had made of men hunting boar, a scene that would last longer than those drawn in the sand by the men. Such visits were always an opportunity for exchanging gifts—gifts that were reminders of the bonds between people. Wealhtheow would never forget where the red fabric came from, and Signy would remember Wealhtheow whenever her eyes fell on that tapestry.

When they reached the harbor, Wealhtheow and Signy embraced, as did their mothers. Hrothgar and Olaf embraced, but then the prince took the princess's hand and kissed it—something that Wealhtheow would never forget.

As they boarded their ship, clouds were just starting to form, so they stayed close to the shoreline as they moved north through the fjord. The men rowed hard as the clouds darkened. Just as they reached the northern tip of Zealand, the first snow started to fall. In the silence of the snowfall camp was quickly set up and a bonfire lit for the night. By the next morning the ground was white but the sky blue and the water calm. The wind was right for their journey down through the strait between Denmark and Scania, past the harbor from which they had departed several days earlier and around the tip of Scania. That evening they arrived happily in the harbor of Olaf's settlement.

7

HEALFDENE'S RETURN
AND SIGNY'S VISIT

We have learned something about travel by sea. King Healfdene's visit to England takes the better part of a year. Once he returns to Denmark, my questions concern what he has learned in England and what others in both Denmark and Scania are to do. My questions are answered while sitting in the posture of the Freyr Diviner. The relationship between Fiona, Signy's guvernante, and Vanadisdottir, Wealhtheow's teacher, is explored using the Freyja Initation posture, illuminating the differences in their beliefs about the gods and goddesses. While standing in the Freyja Initiation posture (see page 96), I ask questions about how these two guvernantes, with their differences in belief, relate to each other and to Signy and Wealhtheow, the two princesses who seem destined to become sisters-in-law.

Healfdene's return from his journey to England brought him as far as the land of the Jutes, the peninsula to the West of Zealand, just as winter was setting in. For this reason he spent this time with these friendly people who for many years have paid him tribute in return for his protection from raiders and invading tribes from the south. Healfdene had brought peace to Juteland, which was now part of the land held by the Skjǫldung. Healfdene was warmly welcomed by the Jute king, Gairvat, the father of Æðelstan. Gairvat was eager for news of his son.

The young Prince Æðelstan, the second son of Gairvat, had wanted to travel and make a name for himself, so three years earlier he had set off to establish a Danish colony in England, where he had declared himself a king.

Healfdene brought his friend some good news. Æðelstan was winning battle after battle against the Angles, he said, with Heorogar as his chief warrior to protect and expand the new settlement. His winter sojourn in Juteland gave Healfdene an opportunity to renew his friendship and strengthen his alliance with the Jutes. By early spring he was ready to return to his home at Hleidargard. Healfdene had been gone a year and was eager to get home. There was much business for him to attend to: assessing the strength of his men, becoming acquainted with new warriors seeking to pledge their allegiance to him, listening to the stories of his heroes, presenting glittering armbands and other gifts for the warriors' heroic acts against raiders of his land, and most of all just spending time with his men to reaffirm his authority in the land.

Seeing her husband arrive home without Heorogar, Sigrid's heart dropped even further. Heorogar felt responsible to his promise to Æðelstan to lead his army against the Angles and to strengthen the fledgling Danish colony of Danelaw in East Anglia, the king told her. The prince had promised to come home the following spring, so he likely had already embarked on his way home by now, Healfdene optimistically added.

Then Sigrid told the king about the visit by Olaf and the sad vision of Olaf's priestess. Though he commiserated with his wife in her grief, he rationalized by telling himself that Vanadisdottir was a priestess of Freyja and he did not believe in the supremacy of that goddess, so the priestess could very well be wrong and Heorogar might very well return despite her prediction. Though Sigrid thought differently she did not speak her thoughts, yet in her confusion she began to cry harder. She hoped the king was right. Meanwhile, Healfdene thought he should pay a visit to Olaf to offer some reassurance that Heorogar was certainly already on his way home, and that Gefjon would not let his first son die. He knew his beliefs differed from those of Olaf who had faith in Vanadisdottir's ability to see and in her faith in Freyja. Yet for the time being he had too much that needed to be done at home right now to make another journey quite so soon.

That spring, however, Signy expressed an urge to visit her new friend Wealhtheow. For months she had been pleading with her mother to allow her to visit the land across the strait, a land that could be seen from their eastern shores. Signy's husband, Sœvil, was again away on the king's business. Now that her father was home, she expressed her desire to visit Scania to him. Signy, who was now sixteen years old, could leave Hrok, her young son, in the care of his wet nurse and her mother, Queen Sigrid. After all, she would be gone only for a few days. Fiona, her guvernante, would accompany her on this trip. In Signy's proposed visit, Healfdene was quick to see an opportunity to solve his dilemma. He told Hrothgar to escort his sister on this trip and carry the news of Heorogar's imminent return to Olaf and thereby reassure him—and Wealhtheow—that the crown prince was certainly already on his way home, and that Gefjon would prevail.

Hrothgar busied himself in preparations for the trip. They would leave the day after tomorrow. Oarsmen were gathered, gifts collected, and baggage and other equipment carried to the harbor at the foot of the fjord. The day of their departure was a pleasant one, with a breeze at their back that made the trip easy. They sailed out of the fjord to the northern tip of Zealand. Rounding the tip, they had to turn their sails, but they caught the wind from the west, which carried them down through the strait. That night they went ashore on the Scania side of the strait and set up camp. The next morning was again clear, with a good wind from the west as they proceeded down through the strait to the southern tip of Scania. Upon turning to the east the oarsmen had to exert themselves with the change in the wind direction, but it was only a short distance until they reached Olaf's settlement by nightfall.

Fiona, Signy's guvernante, was at her side as they came into the estuary. When Olaf's sentry saw them coming in and recognized the banner of Healfdene, he quickly ran to the High Chief with the news that visitors were on their way. This set the settlement in motion in preparation for a welcoming celebration. A delegation left the great hall to escort the guests back up the hill, where they were greeted by Olaf, with Gunheid at his side. Wealhtheow was part of this delegation and was soon at Signy's side. The two princesses chattered nonstop. Signy tried to tell her that Heorogar was well and on his way home from England, but Wealhtheow already knew the truth, had her mind set on Hrothgar and couldn't keep her eyes off him as he walked ahead of them. As they walked and talked, Wealhtheow told her friend that the spring wool market was now in progress, which was obvious from the display of festive banners and stalls along the hillside.

"How could two such special events happen at the very same time—a visit from Signy and the excitement of the wool market?" Vanadisdottir exclaimed. "Hil! Freyja! It is Freyja's love that brings people together like this."

At this exclamation, Signy looked at Fiona, who in turn offered a smile to Vanadisdottir. "I was named Fiona after the goddess Gefjon. We pay homage to Freyja because she helps our mothers in childbirth and helps our gardens, but we believe that Gefjon, with the help of her four sons, is more powerful. Gefjon is the goddess of the Danes. She is the one who brought us our land. She nurtured the infant Scyld Scefing when he was separated from his family as her four oxen sons dragged our land from Sweden. As Scyld Scefing grew and became our first king, she took him as husband and was the mother to our lineage of kings, the Skjǫldung."

Signy added, "We call Gefjon our great-grandmother."

Vanadisdottir returned Fiona's smile. "Thank you for remembering your goddess and namesake. I am sometimes afraid that these stories will be forgotten. If they are, it would be a tragedy for the world."

The royal entourage arrived at the chieftain's great hall in the midst of the excitement of the spring wool market. Colorful pavilions had been set up around the hall and wares set out on blankets. Wool was stacked high on carts and wagons. Holding pens had been set up for the bleating sheep and bellowing rams. As they walked through the aisles of vendors, their eyes were fixed on the activity of the bustling market. The people of the settlement needed more wool after their winter of spinning and weaving. The merchants from the ships in the harbor needed woven fabric, and the freemen from outlying farms needed the tools and wares of the merchants. The blacksmiths of the settlement needed the raw metals brought from the lake district of Sweden by the merchants. Trading was brisk.

Wealhtheow and Signy always had their eyes on the jewelry of the merchants from across the seas and would pause to look as they passed through the aisles. The men of Olaf's welcoming party led the way up to the great hall, with Hrothgar and his men joining them. The aroma of steaming food cooking on the fires around the great hall pulled them onward. When they entered the hall and their eyes adjusted to the dim light, they could see Olaf sitting in his chair with a big grin on his face. Spring and royal visitors made for a joyous time. He came down from his high seat to embrace Hrothgar and beckoned him to sit beside him, ready to hear news of the world beyond the settlement. After Signy received Olaf's greetings, she and Wealhtheow left the great hall and the talk of men to return to the stalls of the vendors outside.

Hearing from Hrothgar the story of Healfdene's trip to England and the delay in Heorogar's return only validated what Olaf already knew with mixed feelings. Inside he was anticipating the joy of Hrothgar sitting next to him as his son-in-law. But this thought was not on Hrothgar's mind—he was expecting his older brother to return. Olaf had learned that Hrothgar was next in line to be the Skjǫldung king, and that his own daughter would be his queen, but he couldn't say anything just yet to the prince seated next to him. The only sure thing was that Signy and Wealhtheow were to be sisters, and this was their time to bond. After all, the purpose of the visit had been to grant Signy's wish to visit Wealhtheow.

The gift exchange during such royal visits happened as part of the evening feastivities in the great hall, but the two princesses couldn't wait that long. They were each proud of their skill in weaving—Wealhtheow of her tapestries, and Signy of her colorful dyed fabrics. They both wanted the other to see what they had done during the winter and had planned on exchanging their weavings. But that is what they had exchanged last fall, and both held what they had received then in special honor. Now they were more excited about the possibility of trading their weavings for broaches and other jewelry of the merchants. They each knew what the other was thinking and readily agreed to trade for what they really wanted—jewelry.

Meanwhile, Fiona and Vanadisdottir were watching their two young charges with affection when suddenly from out of the crowd a young shepherd emerged and threw his arms around Vanadisdottir in an excited embrace. This act and the boy's shocking appearance, with part of his face missing, startled Fiona, who lost her footing as she stepped back. As Vanadisdottir reached out to stop the guvernante from falling, the priestess introduced her to Thord and told Fiona about his special gift of seeing—that he was a natural-born seiðmaðr, or seiðr man. Fiona's mouth dropped open; she didn't know what to think. In her tradition such a person was not trusted.

Vanadisdottir then turned to Thord: "It looks like you have something to tell me."

He nodded.

The priestess looked around for a quiet place to sit and spotted a rönn tree not far away. "Fiona, can you watch over the princesses for a few moments?" And to Thord: "Let's go over there."

Thord was eager to tell her about his experiences with seeing during the previous winter. Vanadisdottir sat listening with her arm around the neck of Heim Thord's loyal hound. The dog had been named after Heimdall, the Vanir god with acute hearing, because of the animal's ability to see and hear what others could not. Thord explained that as each of his ewes had been bred, he had held them in the bear hug shown him by Vanadisdottir. He would then have a vision of how the pregnancy would go. So far this spring, as each lambed he had found that his visions had been correct. For the first six births he knew the number of lambs, whether each was a ewe or a ram, and whether or not they would survive the birthing. He had been right each time. At first he told no one, but after the second ewe gave birth and he found he was correct, he told his father. His father at first just smiled, but as each ewe gave birth, his father began to take notice.

Even more exciting was Thord's vision of his mother giving birth to twin boys. Up until now Thord had been her only child, and his mother and father had counted on twelve-year-old Thord to take over the farm in their old age. His mother had lost several pregnancies, and she was telling no one that she was pregnant again, but Thord knew. He often heard from his father that the steading was to become his. Because he was disfigured, no one believed that he could become anything but a shepherd, and that he probably would never marry either. Now Thord had a new dream—the dream of being a trusted advisor and seer for the king. But who would take over the farmstead? Now he knew that when the twins came of age he would be free to leave the farm to his brothers.

As she talked with Thord, Vanadisdottir watched the two young princesses from a distance as they worked their way down the aisles of vendors. She knew she should soon get back to them. It was not polite to turn her responsibility over to Fiona, as she was also a guest. She asked Thord where he was camping. He replied that he was at the market with his uncle and cousin since his mother was at home, by now very pregnant, and needed his father to be nearby. He pointed to a *hasselnöt,* a hazelnut tree, which could be seen over the top of the vendor's canopies. "We are camping below that tree."

In seeing Thord's excitement he was clearly not invisible, and Vanadisdottir suddenly knew what she needed to teach him next. Because of his appearance, everyone took notice of him. A cat stalking is quiet and its prey does not notice it. It was time for Thord to learn to stalk invisibly. "I am so glad that you are doing well with your visioning. I have much to teach you and will come to find you early tomorrow morning, but I need to get back the princess now. The high chief expects me to be watching her."

When she returned to the girls, Wealhtheow was holding a carved figure of Freyja riding her golden boar, Hildisvíni. She was considering getting it for Signy. She so much wanted her friend to value Frejya as she did. A person could worship more than one god or goddess equally, as she did Freyja and Idunn, she thought. The vendor had overheard the two girls discussing the virtues of Freyja and Gefjon and pulled out of his bag a carved figure of a woman with her arm around the neck of an ox. The woman was Gefjon. When he placed it in Signy's hand, she smiled. Signy wanted the same thing of Wealhtheow—for her to appreciate Gefjon. Fiona, standing nearby, was unsure of this. She did not know if Freyja could be equal to Gefjon. Vanadisdottir reminded Fiona of the realms of the two goddesses separated by the Gorge of Sorrow, Gilharmra, and mentioned that Signy and Wealhtheow wanted to reach across that gorge. The goddesses could be equal, she said, and each had something to teach. The vendor was happy with the weavings the girls presented for trade, and the two future sisters each held a carved goddess that was a valued part of the other's beliefs. They both were ready to learn about and value another goddess.

During that evening's banquet the two young women and their ladies-in-waiting sat together at one table and their conversation continued. Prince Hrothgar and High Chief Olaf exchanged gifts. One gift was a golden helmet that King Healfdene had brought home from his trip to England, which Hrothgar presented to Olaf. Olaf had for Hrothgar a foal from his best mare and a gold armband. Queen Sigrid had sent Olaf's queen a beautiful woven cloak, and in return Hrothgar would take back to his mother a golden broach. In such gift exchanges each tried to outdo the other.

By now the two princesses were open to learning about the other's patroness goddess and were thirsting for stories from their guvernantes. Fiona first told the story of Gefjon's four giant oxen sons—stories of their strength and how the goddess had used them to plow the land from Sweden to form Zealand. Vanadisdottir also knew the stories of Gefjon so added,

"After this land was pulled out to sea and settled next to Juteland, Gefjon discovered an infant lying on the beach at the foot of the fjord where the harbor of Hleidargard is now. She took the baby in her arms and raised him. As he grew, he was much larger and stronger than other children his age. She realized that he could become a powerful man and wanted the best for him, so she asked Odin if he would foster this child. Odin agreed, and as Scyld Scefing grew into manhood he became the first king of Denmark, and hence the beginning of the lineage of Skjǫldung kings. Gefjon then took him as a husband, and their first son was Beow."

The storytelling returned to Fiona, "Scyld Scefing was a benevolent king and protected his own kingdom as well as the lands of his neighbors. Because of this, the kings and chieftains of the surrounding lands paid him tribute. His wealth grew, and when he died Beow became king. He too was powerful and benevolent and loved by everyone. Eventually, his son Healfdene was born. This makes Signy the goddess Gefjon's great-granddaughter, and when you marry the prince your children will be great-great-grandchildren of Gefjon."

Wealhtheow was beginning to feel a closer connection to and greater love for this goddess, knowing that she would be the great-great grandmother of her future children. As the four women then retreated to Wealhtheow's hall for the night, Fiona continued telling the story of how Gefjon took all young women who died as virgins to her realm, Gratabjǫð, the Weeping Fields, and how she would walk among these virgins as they sat beside Harmagil, the Gorge of Sorrow, while they spun and wove, watching the warriors they loved, warriors who died in their first battle, through the yellow smoke and sulfurous fumes rising from Niflheim at the bottom of the gorge, the underworld realm of those who died of illness and old age, the realm ruled by Hel. Thus Wealhtheow fell asleep dreaming of Gefjon and these virgins.

The next morning, Wealhtheow and Signy were contentedly sitting with other women, engaged in spinning and weaving, so Vanadisdottir asked to be excused so that she could visit Thord. She found him beneath the hasselnöt, just finishing breakfast. She beckoned to him to come with her, but before they left his camp she asked him to pick up several hazelnut shells leftover from last fall's crop lying beneath the tree. She then led him down one of the aisles of vendors to a blacksmith's stall. As they stood watching the blacksmith—always a fascinating experience for a young man—she told him to watch out of the corner of his eye the man in the next stall calling out to potential customers to play his shell game.

The priestess spoke in a quiet voice: "You don't want him to take notice of you so pretend you are watching the blacksmith. You need to be invisible to the shell-game man if you want to learn his tricks. You will see things differently by looking out of just the corner of your eye, and what you will see will tell you how he does his tricks. I will leave you here. When you figure his game out, come and find me. You easily found me last night."

Later that morning, Thord found Vanadisdottir. "I figured it out. When the shell man slides the shells around on the table, the stone under the one shell falls off the edge of the table, so when the player chooses a shell nothing is under any of the shells. When the shell man then picks up the shell with the stone under it he really drops a stone on the table as he picks up the shell."

"Good. You're learning to stalk like a cat. It's important to stalk invisibly and it takes a lot of practice. Do you remember the binding that held Fenrir, the wolf son of Loki? The first substance used in making the binding was the sound a cat makes when it walks. That sound is the invisible silence of a cat when it stalks. Now take the shells you picked up this morning and carve them for a shell game. Practice picking up a shell and dropping the stone with one hand so no one will notice you dropping it. When you are sure you know how to do it I want you to play the game, but pick up the shell before the shell man does and drop a stone when you pick it up. That way you will show him you know his trick. He'll let you play only once."

Thord practiced for the rest of the day. Though it looked easy, it was more difficult than he thought. He couldn't just drop the stone because it would roll or bounce away. When uncovering a stone one expects it to be lying under the shell. He had to find a way to press it against the table as he lifted the shell so it would look like it had been lying under the shell. He eventually found that he could roll the stone from the palm of his hand down to the tip of one finger using his thumb while picking up the shell with two fingers, but to do it consistently and smoothly took practice. He went back a couple of times to again watch the shell man to see what fingers he used to roll the stone and pick up the shell, and he finally got it.

The next morning Thord went back to play the shell game. He put his coin on the table and the shell man matched it. When the shell man saw the stone under the shell that Thord lifted, he smiled and waved him away, knowing that he had figured out the game. Thord walked away with two coins. The next player played and lost but wanted to try again. Again he lost. He shook his head, and as he walked away he asked Thord how he did it. Thord just smiled and walked on. He didn't want to make an enemy of the shell man. Another part of the trick that Thord learned was that the player usually didn't pick up the shell, but the shell man was quick to reach for and pick up the shell the player pointed to. It might have been then that the stone under the shell disappeared. He always tipped the top of the shell toward the player as he picked it up.

Thord walked on to explore more of the market. He found a magician performing and stopped to watch awhile, this time stalking like a cat. There he did not have to pretend to be watching something else because he was part of an audience watching the magician. Yet he learned how important it was to watch how the magician moved his fingers. It was these movements that often gave away the trick.

That afternoon the vendors began packing up their wares. Thord's wool and three young lambs had been traded with the help of his uncle.

Thord was going home with what his family needed, the most important item being an iron cauldron and an ax head, because all the nearby farmsteads were small and none had a blacksmith. He was also taking back some spices for cooking and a broach for his mother, among other things. Before he left he went to find Vanadisdottir to tell her about his success. He found her once again walking with the two princesses and Fiona.

The two girls were talking about Freyja and the two guvernantes' bedtime stories of the previous night. Signy was curious about Sweden's other large lake and asked Vanadisdottir how Lake Vättern, was formed. This was a story that Wealhtheow had heard many times but she always enjoyed hearing it again, and this time she enjoyed watching Signy listening to the story that Vanadisdottir told:

"Last night you heard how Gefjon plowed the land from Sweden to form Zealand and made Sweden's largest lake, Vänern. Freyja made Lake Vättern. It was at the foot of this lake that I was trained to be a priestess. Well, Freyja was married to Odr, and they had two daughters, Hnoss and Gersimi. But Odr was a wanderer, always wanting to see new parts of the world. When he left Freyja, she cried tears of gold, knowing that he would not return. She longed to see him and would sit on her seiðr platform searching for him. Their daughters would do the same thing, also searching for their father. One day when Freyja was out brushing her golden boar, Hildisvini, Frigg came running up to tell her that she had just seen Odr from her seiðhjallr walking down through Sweden. Freyja had a good feeling that this might be the day she would find him, so she was quick to jump on her boar, and she took off and flew down along central Sweden. It was not long before she found what she thought was Odr. She pulled hard on her reins and Hildisvini put his butt down and his feet out in front of him to come to a skidding stop. As he skidded, the boar dug a long trench, pushing the dirt ahead of him, thus forming Lake Vättern. But to Freyja's sadness she did not find Odr. As she cried, her tears fell to the ground, forming the many dark pools of water, or helgatjörn, found so plentifully south of the lake.

It was beside one of these tarns of Freyja that I was trained to be her priestess."

That night at bedtime Signy questioned Vanadisdottir. "Tell us about your training."

"Well, just for a little while. You need to get to sleep . . . When my father died, my mother could not take care of three daughters, so she sent me to the sacred pool of Freyja to be trained. I was the oldest and was more ready to leave home. I spent six years there. There were twenty-four young women novices. Three other girls started there the same time I did. The four of us spent our first year caring for the needs of the others, washing their clothes and taking out and dumping the morning buckets. It was during the second year that we started learning the magic of stalking like a cat and the compassion of Freyja, and only in our third year did we start to learn the practice of seiðr. I will never forget my sisters of the sacred pool. Now one of those sisters is the high priestess of Freyja. It was so good to visit her two summers ago. Well, now it is time to go to sleep." Vanadisdottir kissed each girl on the forehead and then lay down herself.

Signy was beginning to take a real interest in Freyja and Vanadisdottir, while Wealhtheow was interested and asking questions about Gefjon. Both guvernantes were enjoying showing their knowledge of the two goddesses and feeling close to each other as they felt close to the two girls.

The next day was the last day of the market, so the two girls and their guvernantes wanted to take one last walk through the aisles of the vendors. It was then that Thord found Vanadisdottir. This time the priestess told the girls a bit more about Thord and his ability to see and that he was now learning to stalk like a cat. Knowing this made the girls feel closer to this young man, as hideous as he might look. Wealhtheow asked him, "Are you going to go away to be trained for six years? Is that how men are trained to be priests? For what god will you be a priest?"

Vanadisdottir interrupted: "That's a lot of questions. I don't think he knows yet. He has a few years before his brothers are old enough to do the farm work so that he can get away for such training. Those are important questions for Thord to be thinking about." She then turned to Thord, "You have a lot of work to do for your family. During the winter you learned a lot on your own. With what I taught you here about stalking like a cat, the more you stalk, just stalking everything around you, the more you will learn. Last night I had a vision that I will be seeing you again before this next winter. Practice making spirit journeys like you did in finding your neighbor's ram. I think it might be on one of these journeys that we might meet again. That will be the time to take the next step." With that, she embraced the young man and reminded him that there was a lot he had to do to pack up before he started his journey home.

Thord had to ask, "How? No one can see me when I make a spirit journey."

"You will see and learn. If you meet me while I am on a spirit journey too, we can see, talk to, and touch each other, like when Nanna lived with the Vanir and Baldr with the Æsir—living apart they were really together all the time. I know priestesses who can journey together in this way," though Vanadisdottir had to admit privately that so far she had been unable to do it herself.

With that answer, Thord ran off, grinning widely.

The next morning, Hrothgar, Signy, and Fiona were to leave to return to Zealand. That night the two princesses wanted to hear the story of how Nanna and Baldr were together even though they lived apart. Vanadisdottir indulged their request:

"It was when Moðir was still alive among the Vanir. Frigg wanted to visit the Great Mother, and Baldr asked to go along. It thrilled Frigg that her son wanted to meet Moðir, though he had seen her many times on his spirit journeys. It was during that visit that Baldr met and fell in love with Nanna, a goddess of the Vanir, and before he had to return to the Æsir he and Nanna were married and she became pregnant with Forseti. They were both very skilled in the practice of seiðr and knew that they could be together any time they wanted. In this way they were together so much of the time. Though Forseti lived with his mother among the Vanir when he was very young, Nanna could take him to see his father simply by holding his hand when she journeyed to see him. By the time Forseti was old enough and wanted to live with his father, he had learned to journey on his own and would visit his mother frequently. It was then that the gods and goddesses learned that they did not have to be apart. Life for the Vanir was beautiful with the magical compassion, creativity, and innocence of Moðir, the Great Mother."

The next morning, the Danes' ship was loaded, and after embracing her friends while shedding happy tears, with Hrothgar again kissing Wealhtheow's hand and her blushing at his touch, Signy left with her guvernante, Fiona, with Hrothgar in command.

8

THE RAID

At this point I go back to asking my favorite general question, "What happens next?" What is revealed is an incident that leads to Thord becoming a central figure in this unfolding narrative. My questions as to how Thord is going to handle his gifts, including his extraordinary ability to see, and whether or not King Olaf and others will believe and trust in his powers, are answered while I rest in the Freyr Diviner posture . . .

King Olaf maintained a harbor outpost on the western coast of Scania, at the west harbor, with two ships and twenty men. Many years in the future this harbor would be known as the port city of Malmö, Sweden. In this little settlement there were a number of buildings for the men and their families. From there the sentry could see across the strait and spot any ships that might be coming through the strait between Denmark and Scania. It was this strait that made the alliance between Olaf and Healfdene strategic in controlling the trade flowing from the west and the east.

Fall and Winter had passed and Spring had arrived, a pleasant time of year, as the days were growing longer. The men in all the settlements practiced with their swords and other weapons, while the women spun wool and did their weaving. Life went on uneventfully until one morning a young boy came running into the harbor, breathless, panicked, and in tears. There had been a raid of a steading up the coast. All his family had been killed and the steading had been set on fire. The boy had been up on the hill tending their sheep when he saw a ship coming from the north pull up on the beach near the farm. He said that there were nearly as many men as all of his fingers twice. When the raiders saw the sheep on the hill a couple of them came running toward him. He ran into the woods and came to the harbor as fast as he could. Despite his young age, he prided himself on being a swift runner.

A messenger was sent on horseback to King Olaf while the rest of the men at the harbor grabbed their weapons and ran to a readied ship on the beach. They were off in only a few minutes, rowing hard up the coast. The air was still and they soon could see smoke rising straight into the air. As they approached the farmstead there was no sign of life in the water or on the land. The men wasted no time and continued up the coast. As they came around the next point of land, the water opened out in front of them and as far as they could see there was no sign of a ship. The raiders must have pulled in somewhere. The coast was long on both sides of the strait; it would take days to search the coast, but from this point a ship could be seen as it pulled away from the shore, so there they set up camp to wait and watch.

That same morning, on his farmstead north of the settlement of King Olaf, Thord awakened from a nightmare. He was breathing heavily and was wet from sweat. He saw a raider ship coming from the north and pulling ashore near a farmstead. He saw the raiders kill the family and the farmhands, taking everything they could find back to their ship and setting fire to the buildings. On the hill he could see a young boy watching the sheep and a couple of the raiders running up the hill. The boy was quick to disappear into the woods, but the raiders killed several of the sheep and dragged them back down to their boat. They then left, going back up the coast to pull their ship into the inlet of a small river, where they set up camp.

Thord rolled over on his stomach and stretched his arms out in front of him with his ankles crossed. This way, when he moved his attention to his center of harmony, he could leave his body and go on a spirit journey.* He had tried this posture many times before and had been able to see his father working in the fields or his herd of sheep from a bird's-eye vantage point. But he had never gone much beyond his own farm. Often he would find himself going into a cave since this posture is an underworld posture, but that was the only way he could leave his body. There was never any need for him to travel farther, though Thord would soon learn a posture that would allow him to travel great distances.

This time it took Thord no time at all before he journeyed to the coastal farmstead that was burning. Thord knew he had to do something, but there was nothing he could do there, so he willed himself to go to King Olaf's settlement. Energy was in the air for his journey; if only the priestess was on a spirit journey, too, but he saw her out picking plants in the fields instead. She had gotten up early and could not see him.

Thord came out of his trance journey and knew he had to do something, and there was only one thing he could do. He had to get to King Olaf as fast as he could. If he were to tell his father why he needed to go, his father would only tell him he was having a nightmare and would not let him leave the steading. Instead, Thord ran to his horse, mounted, and quietly rode off with his dog, Heim, at his heels.

He rode first to his uncle's steading to find his cousin. He could tell his cousin what he had seen. He didn't know if his cousin would believe him, but he was always ready for an adventure. On the way there, Thord hatched a plan: he would ask his cousin to tell his mother, Thord's aunt, that he was needed today to help Thord and his uncle on their farm. His cousin would then tell his uncle, Thord's father, that Thord had left to tell King Olaf his dream. By then Thord would be well on his way to the king's settlement.

It took Thord the better part of a day to reach the settlement, but he arrived before the messenger from the west harbor did. He first went

---

*See "The Sami Lower World Posture," page 19.

to find the one ally he had in the settlement, Vanadisdottir, to tell her his story. She immediately took him to the king. Olaf listened, but with some skepticism, but soon the messenger from the harbor came running in with the same story. Olaf's eyes grew big as he looked back at Thord. When Thord told him where the raiders were camping, the messenger knew the very spot.

Olaf's chief retainer, Hailgesson, "the son of Hailgair," sat in the place of honor at the foot of the king. He quickly had two ships readied and his party of warriors pushed off through the estuary leading out to the sea. It would take them until the next morning to reach the west harbor. Night was short at this time of the year, and there was a nearly full moon.

The other ship's crew continued to stand vigil on the point above the west harbor. They still didn't see the ship of the raiders, but did see a column of smoke rising in the still morning air and thought it could be the raiders' camp. The best they could do at this time was to stay where they were on the point. If they went to find the camp and they were wrong, the raiders might escape without being seen. From where the men stood now, no one could escape their notice.

By the next morning they saw the king's two ships coming up past the harbor. With three ships, two of them captained by Hailgesson, they could attack the camp. The smoke was coming from where Thord, in his vision, had last seen the raiders. The two crews rowed up the inlet, into the mouth of a stream. They proceeded upstream, and as the water became shallower they saw what they were looking for: the raider's ship resting under an overhanging tree. The shouts of the raiders could be heard as they prepared to fight to protect their ship, their only lifeline to home. Hailgesson's fighting men, thirty in all, swarmed ashore a short distance below the camp. As they moved through the brush and woods, the fighting began. Two of Hailgesson's men waded through the water and along the bank to duck behind the raider's ship and pull it away from the bank. The raiders were not greatly skilled with sword and spear and were soon vanquished. Their ship, loaded with the spoils of their raids, including one prisoner, was taken back to the harbor.

Meanwhile, the women of the harbor settlement had taken in Dan, the young farm boy whose family had been murdered by the raiders, and were comforting him. When the three ships entered the harbor, everyone ran to the water's edge. When Dan saw the raiders' ship again, loaded up with goods and animals stolen not only from his family's farmstead, but those of other farmsteads up the coast, he burst into a new round of crying.

Olaf and six of his retainers left that night, riding across the well-worn path to the west harbor, arriving before his ships returned. The man whom the raiders had taken prisoner was questioned. Olaf's men learned what they already suspected: that the raiders were from Norway. No Danes would have attacked their own farms. Olaf praised the valor of his men and promised them gifts for their victory when they returned to the settlement to celebrate.

Back at the king's settlement, Thord, Vanadisdottir, and Wealhtheow sat under the shade of the thatched pavilion, talking. Thord said, "I keep telling this story over and over. My dream, my spirit journey, and what really happened were all the same."

"Thord, you have special powers," said Vanadisdottir. "You have one good eye, but people who are blind often have an amazing power to see—to see what others cannot see. You have that power. And it didn't take you six years of training like it took me to discover this gift."

"But what do I do now?" he asked. "When I am on the hill with my sheep, I can leave my body to watch my father working in the fields, or I can see myself and the sheep from high above. But I could never go much farther than the farm until this morning."

"The raid gave off an energy that pulled you to it," Vanadisdottir explained. "It was something that you had to see. It was something that has changed your life."

"I know. When I stop to think about it, it scares me. I like it on the hillside with my sheep. It's peaceful there. There I can dream about exciting things, but I don't think of them as real, at least not yet. The raid was real. I used to dream of being a warrior, fighting raiders. That is what my father wanted me to be. But without my eye I know I can't be a great warrior. But I can be a farmer and a shepherd, and I now dream of such things. I know I have a few years before my brothers are old enough for me to leave the farm, but what if there is another raid and I have another nightmare, and I have to ride hard to get to the settlement to warn everyone?"

"You can do just that."

"It would have been better if I could have warned them quicker. You said yourself that if you had been on a spirit journey at the same time I was, I could have told you, and you would have heard me. But you weren't journeying, you were in the fields picking herbs. You didn't have a nightmare about the raid."

Vanadisdottir thought a moment. "There have been other raids, and it is true, I have never had a dream about them. My dreams and visions are about healing and teaching people, like the vision I had that led me to teach you. The gods and goddesses each have different powers—they are not all the same. That's why I love Freyja and Idunn so much. Their powers are of visions of healing, but they are different types of powers. Freyja practices seiðr to make journeys to help and heal others. Idunn can hold plants to her heart and learn how they heal."

"But what gods and goddesses can I learn from?" Thord asked. "What gods will *I* learn to love?"

"That's why it is important to hear the stories of the gods and goddesses," Vanadisdottir replied. "Freyr would journey to watch battles from above, sometimes riding his battle boar, other times using the practice of seiðr like you did this morning. He learned from Bragi how to sing spells to make things happen in the battle, though he would never start a battle. Forseti was good at talking to people in a compassionate way to help them solve problems, and in this way bring peace."

"But where do I learn from the gods? I don't know of any men, any priests of those gods to teach me."

"The seiðr men I've known—and there are not many—have all been like you. They learned from their own experiences. Stalking like a cat was the most important first step. From there they would learn from every experience. Most of them—maybe all of them—wanted at first to be warriors, but because of some physical problem that made it impossible, they learned magical skills."

"But what do I do now?"

"I had a vision after you talked to the king this morning, a vision of the shepherd boy who lost his family, a vision of your family taking him in and of you staying here in the settlement. You can be fostered by the king and I can teach you. I can tell you the stories of the gods. You can stalk and learn from your experiences and find the gods you love. You can still be a shepherd right here, close by, and when you have nightmares we will listen."

"I don't know if my family is ready for that. I'm sure they are worried about me right now," Thord said.

"We will talk with the king when he gets back from the west harbor. I'm sure when your parents hear the story of what happened they will be proud of you."

No one had thought about how worried Thord's parents might be. Wealhtheow suggested, "We can talk with my mother. She could send someone to tell his parents that everything is alright, and that Thord is now a hero."

Gunheid, Olaf's queen, understanding how parents worry, sent one of the men who had stayed back to protect the settlement to take the news of what had happened to Thord's family, and to tell them that someone from the settlement would bring him home in a couple of days. Wealhtheow also told Gunheid about the priestess's vision for Thord.

It was not until the next day that Olaf came riding in with his retainers. The orphaned boy, Dan, was riding with Hailgesson, the leader of Olaf's warriors, on Hailgesson's horse. Hailgesson asked his wife to care for Dan while he and his men retreated to the great hall, and to their positions close to the king. There a horn of mead was passed around while the men talked about the events of the past day.

Olaf had not yet entered the hall and was in Gunheid's hall, where he was treating her to the story of the demise of the raiders and the capture of their ship loaded with plunder. He praised Thord in directly leading his men to the raiders' camp. Gunheid told him of Vanadisdottir's vision of Thord staying near the settlement, and the young shepherd, Dan, being fostered by Thord's parents.

When Olaf entered the great hall he called for Hailgesson to bring him Dan and Thord. The two shepherd boys then met. Olaf suggested that now that Dan was without a family, Thord's family could foster him, and that he himself would be pleased to become Thord's foster father, and that Thord could serve as a shepherd to the flock of sheep near the settlement. That way he would be close by to help the king with his power of seeing, and Vanadisdottir could tell him the stories of the gods that would help him in his training. That plan seemed to make sense to everybody. The king added that tomorrow he would take the boys to the farmstead to ask Thord's parents for their approval of this plan, but tonight the two boys—these two heroes—were to be in the great hall to celebrate.

That evening the two boys sat at the head table, at the feet of the king. They ate heartily, and when Olaf started bestowing gifts on his men, both boys received their first armbands—Dan for escaping the raiders and bringing the news of the raid to the men at the harbor, and Thord for his vision of what had happened and the raiders' location. The king comforted Dan for the loss of his family and hoped that he could find some consolation in wearing the armband of a hero.

The next morning, Olaf and six of his men and the two boys rode off to the north. By early afternoon they arrived at Thord's family's steading, where Thord was reunited with his parents. The king presented his case eloquently for wanting to foster Thord at the settlement, and for Dan being fostered on the farmstead. How could a family deny such a request from their king? They would be proud of their son living in the household of the king, and for them it would be a pleasure and honor to foster a strong young lad like Dan. Thus all agreed. After a simple farmer's meal, during which Olaf heard about the life of a farm family at the edge of his realm, the king was offered Thord's bed, while the two youths bedded down in the fresh hay of the barn with the king's six retainers.

The next morning, on their return trip to Olaf's hall, the entourage stopped at the farm of Thord's cousin so that Thord could tell him the news of all that had happened, to show him his armband, and to thank him for the role he had played in catching the raiders. The group arrived back at the southern tip of Scania and the now-quiet settlement by the middle of the afternoon.

9

NEWS FROM ENGLAND

News of the demise of the Danish settlement in England reaches Denmark and Scania, and questions arise regarding what happens next. King Olaf and his daughter, Wealhtheow, decide to travel to Denmark to express their condolences to King Healfdene and Queen Sigrid. Ecstatic journeying, this time in the Hallstatt Warrior posture, tells me where people go after death. I personally find certain postures particularly powerful and the Hallstatt Warrior posture has been especially powerful to me in journeying back through time.

It soon becomes apparent that King Healfdene does not believe in the seiðmaðr's magical powers of seeing. This underscores the differences in the beliefs of the two royal families with regard to the Nordic gods and goddesses, and the skepticism that each family has of the other's beliefs. These differences will have to be dealt with as these two families come together in their grief. I receive answers to my questions about the different belief systems of the two families by using both the Freyr Diviner and the Realm of the Dead postures.

Meanwhile, the story of Breca that is passed through dreaming from Thord to Vanadisdottir comes at an opportune time, to eventually sway Healfdene to finally accept the powers of the young seiðmaðr. I also ask questions of Freyr regarding Vanadisdottir's training of Thord and what will be the next step for this gifted young man . . .

The Hallstatt Warrior Posture*

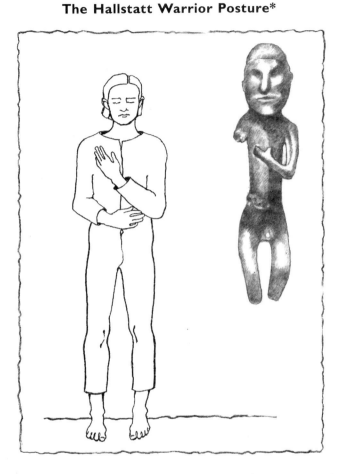

Stand with your feet about five inches apart and your toes pointed forward. Your knees may be slightly bent, as in the Danish figure (to the right in the illustration), or locked, as in the Hallstatt Warrior. Place your right arm along your waist with the palm of your hand covering your navel. Your left upper arm rests alongside your torso, with the left hand resting on your right breast, with your fingers pointing toward the right shoulder. The Hallstatt Warrior shows more tension in the shoulders than does the Danish version of this posture. Your face is forward with eyes closed.

---

*This posture is also known as the Danish Realm of the Dead posture.

The rest of that spring was peaceful, with no more raids, and so Thord slept peacefully each night in the hall of the king. He spent his days on the hillside tending the settlement's sheep, and this is where Vanadisdottir would find him to tell him the stories of the gods. Sometimes the princess would join them to hear the stories, too.

There was still talk of the raid. The man who'd been taken prisoner by the raiders was put to work in the settlement as a woodcutter. He told the people that the raiders had camped where they did because it was not far from a farm they had destroyed a couple of days earlier. Hidden in the woods close to the water, and with no one around, they thought they would be safe. Everyone agreed that the raiders were not very smart in leaving themselves so vulnerable and showing the world where they were with the smoke from their campfire.

Spring moved into summer, and a merchant ship arrived with the news that didn't surprise Wealhtheow—news of the death of Heorogar. The previous fall, the tribes of East Anglia had organized to protect their land and had laid siege to the Danish settlement. Æðelstan and his men, led by Heorogar, had fought valiantly, but in the end all died in battle. No specific mention was made of Wealhtheow's brother, Olfdene, but it was assumed he had died, too, since the merchant had heard of no survivors or captives. The Danish settlement in England had been short-lived. The king and queen and Wealhtheow grieved the death of Olfdene in private, since for rest of the settlement he had been forgotten, as they did not know of his whereabouts.

Vanadisdottir had another vision. She knew that Æðestan had carried with him an *ask,* or ash tree, to plant in their colony in England. He took this Tree of Life symbol to represent their roots in Denmark, the roots of the Skjǫldung. The priestess's vision was of this tree as it grew for many years. The people of England and Denmark soon would forget about its beginning. She then saw a Danish ship land on the coast of England and a new settlement being formed. A great hall in the center of the settlement was built, and the *ask* tree was cut down for the central pole of the hall. In the vision she saw the rings of the tree and knew there were 300. She then knew that it would not be for another 300 years that the Danes would have a permanent settlement in that distant land across the sea.

With the news that the merchant brought of the demise of the Danish settlement and the death of all its warriors, Olaf affirmed that he must go to Healfdene to express his condolences to the king and his family. Olaf, Gunheid, and Wealhtheow prepared to leave, along with twelve men. Before their departure Vanadisdottir asked Gunheid for something that belonged to Olfdene. The queen came back with a clasp from his cloak. Then the priestess, Gunheid, and Wealhtheow all went east along the shore a short distance, to a small ravine that ran down to the boggy edge of the estuary. There, on the edge of the bog, a place of Freyja and her father, Njord, who loved the edge of the sea, they made a stacked stone altar and placed the cloak clasp on top with a prayer to Freyja that she would take Olfdene to her realm at the Cliff of Lucklessness, Gæfuleysabjarg. Vanadisdottir hoped that Olfdene had heard enough of the stories of the Vanir that he would know from there how to find his way to the Dwelling Place of Peace, Griðbustaðr, the place where those who understand and practice the compassionate magic of the Vanir reside. Soon the clasp of Olfdene's cloak would be washed into the sacred depths of the bog. They then left for Hleidargard.

The winds were calm on the journey to Hleidargard, and it took the oarsmen four days to reach the foot of Healfdene's fjord. When they arrived at the settlement they were greeted by the sorrowing royal family, and heartfelt condolences were expressed. Olaf and Wealhtheow were taken out into a field where there was a large burned area with some still-smoldering wood. This is where the mourners had built a sacred fire to send any remaining belongings of Heorogar and other sacrifices made in his name to Odin, since Heorogar's body had not been returned from England for a proper ship burial, which is the Nordic tradition. Olaf had brought Olfdene's sword for this sacrifice, a sword that might have been used to fight alongside Heorogar if he would have been allowed to take it to England. Olaf pulled together some of the embers of the fire and placed the beloved sword on the fire, as much for Olfdene as for Heorogar, knowing that the two warriors had become friends—a story he could not tell Healfdene or anyone else since Olfdene, having been exiled, was supposed to have been forgotten. Olaf and Wealhtheow together placed an armband in the fire to honor Heorogar, a great warrior, the first-born prince who would have been Wealhtheow's husband. They then returned to the great hall. At the evening meal the horn of mead was passed around, with "Hil! Odin!" shouted in Heorogar's memory.

Wealhtheow retreated to Signy's hall to be with her friend. The two young women and their guvernantes spent the rest of the evening together. Hrok, Signy's child, now a toddler, was scampering around the hall. When food was served, Queen Sigrid joined them. Wealhtheow's betrothal to Hrothgar was appropriately not mentioned; the talk was of Heorogar's journey to Valhalla, and there living the life of a great warrior.

The next day, Olaf told Healfdene the story of the raid that had taken place in Scania the previous spring. Healfdene was a king who valued strength and valor, though he was also gentle and just with the people of his domain. Yet he seemed uneasy when Olaf told him about the visions of Thord and Vanadisdottir. Seiðmaðr—men who practice seiðr—were rumored to be evil, although he himself knew of no such men. That evening in their private quarters Healfdene and Sigrid spoke of seiðmaðr. The queen's comment was, "What do you expect of men who value only physical strength and valor? Your warriors wouldn't understand the sensitivity and magic of a seiðmaðr. The merchant who told us about Heorogar's death told me something else when we were talking: that the kings of England and Ireland have in their courts such men to advise them in warfare and in making other such decisions. They have learned to value seiðmaðr, or as they call, them, Druids."

In Princess Signy's quarters, when Wealhtheow shared the same stories with Signy and her guvernante, Fiona, they were fascinated. How could such a young boy have this gift of the power of vision? Didn't it take a lot of training?

Healfdene and Olaf discussed how they could better protect the strait. Though Healfdene had a harbor to the east on the strait, it was not regularly used because traveling across the swampy land from Hleidargard to the coast was difficult for most of the year. With an alliance between Denmark and Scania, patrolling the strait was more important. The straits between the other islands and Juteland had harbors and were regularly protected by his retainers. They decided that it was important to have a permanent force of men at their harbor to the east. The advantage of having the men there, across from the harbor, so that signal fires could be seen from each shoreline, was acknowledged by King Healfdene and Olaf. This way passage through the strait could be controlled. During the wet season travel to the harbor could be by ship around the northern tip of Denmark, but it was also decided that a land path from Hleidargard to the harbor would be wise, and that the best path needed to be determined, with a couple of outposts established for the relay of men on horseback. This land was considered generally inaccessible and inhabited by outlaws. It was land that could be farmed and needed to be civilized. It was this kind of talk between kings and their chieftains that resulted in the kinds of decisions that gave the Skjǫldung king his strength.

That night, after Vanadisdottir and Fiona told their charges bedtime stories of the goddesses and the young women had fallen asleep, Vanadisdottir had a dream about Thord. In the dream he was trying to reach her to tell her what had happened in the settlement. One of Olaf's retainers had found the body of a man washed ashore just to the east of the settlement. He was still alive, though barely, and had a wound on his leg and had lost a lot of blood. She could help bring him back to health if she were back home in Scania. In her dream she told Thord how to make a compress of kulsukker, or comfrey, and hjulkrone, or borage, to place on the wound. She knew that those plants were plentiful in the area and knew that Thord would recognize them. She also told him to wrap the man in blankets to keep him warm, and if he was awake enough to swallow, to give him some warm tea. Thord then left to do just that. He had received her message through dreaming.

Later that same night, the priestess had another dream about Thord, who told her that the man was awake and had drunk some tea. He was able to talk a little and said his name was Breca, and that he was swimming in a race with another man across the strait from Denmark and around the tip of Scania. The water had gotten rough and he had lost sight of the man he was racing.

The next morning, Vanadisdottir told Queen Sigrid about the two dreams, and the story spread, first to Olaf, and then to Healfdene. Healfdene knew of a giant of a man, a Jute with the same name who the king thought would do something as foolish as swimming across the strait in such a race. He was always challenging others to test his strength against them in all different kinds of contests. At the same time, Healfdene just laughed at the dream.

Olaf was not yet ready to end his visit and leave for home. He was looking forward to spending some time hunting with Healfdene and his men, but at the same time he was very curious about what he would find when he got home—if he would find a swimmer named Breca. Trusting the priestess and Thord, he thought there was a good chance that he would. Vanadisdottir had complete faith in Thord and did not feel it necessary to push the others into leaving for home so early. So they stayed. The next two days were pleasant ones, with the men hunting and the women visiting while doing their spinning and weaving. Though there was some afternoon rain, no one complained. The following morning, Olaf's ship was packed, and the visitors from Scania pushed off to sea. Three days later, after an uneventful trip, they came ashore in the harbor of King Olaf's settlement.

Thord had seen the ship coming around the end of the land and came down from the hill where he was tending sheep to greet Vanadisdottir and to tell her the story of the man who was washed ashore almost a week earlier. He was doing fine. He had quickly regained his strength and was already challenging all of Olaf's warriors to duels with swords, spears, or wrestling matches. He was large and powerful and generally won in almost any kind of competition, but he was so jovial that the king's retainers did not mind losing to him. He gave them a good opportunity to practice their skills and never seemed to tire in such combat.

Olaf wished that his friend, the doubting Healfdene, had been there to see for himself the truth of the priestess's dream of instructing Thord in healing this powerful man from Juteland. Breca was still a young man, out for adventure, but after a few more days in the settlement he was ready to leave for home. Besides fighting and swimming, he also prided himself in being a swift runner. He had heard of the west harbor and challenged King Olaf's men, looking for someone who would race him on foot across the land to that harbor. Olaf assured him that when on his way home, if he would stop to tell King Healfdene about his swimming adventure and subsequent healing by Thord, his men at the harbor would take him across the strait to Denmark, to the king. Because there were no marathon runners among Olaf's warriors, Brecca agreed to race against four of them running in a relay.

On the day of the race, three of the four relay runners left early on horseback to their respective starting positions, dividing the distance into approximately four equal segments for the relay. The fourth and last man was Olaf's swiftest runner. Breca was quite a distance ahead of the first runner by the time that man reached the second runner, at which point Breca was soon out of sight. But the second runner was strong and soon shortened the distance to where he could at least see Breca ahead of him. Yet about halfway to the third runner the distance between the second runner and Breca again started to increase. The third runner did about as well, first closing the gap for a short distance before it started to lengthen again. Finally, with a tag from the third runner, the fourth runner started, and the gap again began to close. By the time they reached the west harbor everyone waiting at the finish line was cheering because both men could be seen in the final stretch, and although the race was close, Breca came out ahead.

Olaf had watched the race from horseback as he rode along the trail to the west harbor. That evening was spent in festivity, with everyone wishing this amiable giant of a man the best. The four relay runners felt no resentment in their loss, as they had enjoyed the competition and the celebration that followed. The next morning a ship was ready to take Breca across the strait. He put himself to the oars along with the other men since there was no wind. As they proceeded across the strait, the other oarsmen began lifting their oars out of the water just to see how strong Breca was in rowing. When they had all raised their oars and only Brecca was rowing, they found that the ship was moving just as fast as it was when the others were helping. Seeing the big grin on Breca's face, all the other men could not help but smile and laugh along with him. Upon reaching shore, before Breca took off across the land toward Hleidargard, he assured the men that he would share his story with Healfdene. And as this story was passed down through future generations, it came to pass that only one person would be able to beat Breca in swimming, and that was the Geat warrior Beowulf, who swam right past Olaf's settlement and found his finish line in Finland.

As for Healfdene, following Brecca's visit the king gained a healthy respect for the practice and power of seiðr. And with the coming together of the two families through the marriage of Wealhtheow and Hrothgar, Vanadisdottir would be part of the dynasty, and the power and love of Freyja would add to the strength of the Skjǫldung.

Vanadisdottir was pleased and excited that she and Thord had been successful in connecting with each other through dreaming. Though she knew of others who were able to do this, it was the first time that she had experienced this form of seiðr, in which another person had met her in her dreaming and responded. After she returned to Scania and talked with Thord she verified that what had happened in her dreaming was true. She also felt that Thord had done an excellent job in ministering to Breca, but she realized it was time to teach him one more aspect of seiðr—the power of the word or song, which was taught by the god Bragi. The priestess busied herself with hollowing out a piece of wood to make him a drum. When it came time for her to prepare the drum head with a piece of rawhide, she cut it to the right size, punched holes along the edge, and cut strips of hide to bind it to the wood. She was then ready to make a sacred drum for her protégé.

She told Thord that they needed to meet by the pond that had become sacred to her, which was near the bastu, the sauna. There she began telling him the story of Bragi and the power of his poetry and song while she made the drum, beginning with soaking the rawhide in the water of the pond. When it was well saturated she laid it across the hollow of the wood, laced it to the wood with hide strips, and then laid it in the sun to dry. As she continued telling the story of Bragi, she taught him her favorite song, "Plants of the Mother":

Listen to the plants   *Listen to the Mother*
The plants of the Mother   *Make us well*
Listen to the plants   *Listen to the Mother*
Use these plants   *To keep us well*

It was an easy song to learn, and when she was making her medicinal potions or ministering to the sick or wounded, she would sing it over and over, quietly, to herself. When her hands were free and she was watching her patient she would recite this song as a poem while beating its rhythm on her drum. Thord had seen her do this. She explained how the drum cleared the mind of other thoughts and allowed the words to enter a cleansed mind, both hers and the patient's. This cleansed mind was a state of trance, a healing trance. The beat of the drum added to the magic of the poetic words. Since Thord's drum was still drying, she demonstrated this mind-cleansing ritual to Thord using her own drum. Since he was healthy, she changed the words slightly, from "make us well" to "keep us well," and from "make us strong" to "keep us strong." There were many situations when it was important for her patients to feel a sense of inner strength, and changing the words in this way would help them feel strong inside. Following this teaching, Thord hung his sacred drum in his hut with a feeling of strength and pride. When the drum was finished it was small enough for him to easily carry it over his shoulder, and it had a beautiful resonant sound. Vanadisdottir told Thord that during the summer, when the air was quite humid, he would need to warm the drum head over a fire to dry the skin enough to bring out the resonant sound.

10

THE PROMISE OF MARRIAGE

It is now time to move on in life following the death of Heorogar. I ask the question, "What are the traditions around the mourning of a loved one—when does the mourning period end, and when is the time right for a marriage?" Apparently, the time was right, because the story flows right into the narrative of the visit by Healfdene to Scania to arrange the marriage of his son to Wealhtheow. Journeying with the Freyja Initiation posture, I uncover details about the ancient Nordic rite of bethrothal. The Freyr Diviner posture brings a vision of the new alliance between Healfdene and Olaf and their plans to protect the straits between their two domains . . .

The following spring, when Wealhtheow was fourteen years old, the regal prow of Healfdene's ship again came into the estuary of Olaf's settlement. The Skjǫldung king, queen, and their daughter, the princess, had come to pay a very special visit to Wealhtheow and her family. Signy's son, Hrok, and his guvernante had come too. It was time for Healfdene to find a wife for his son and heir, Hrothgar.

Hrothgar had remained at home to lead the king's men in protecting Hleidargard. It was better that he not be present while the king negotiated his son's future. The reunion of the two families on this particular occasion was a time of special excitement. Wealhtheow and

Signy were quick to retreat to a place where they could talk and visit, while the king made his formal request for the hand of Olaf's daughter on behalf of Hrothgar. Queen Sigrid had proposed this arrangement the previous year, while Healfdene was away in England, when she first heard the prediction of Heorogar's death, but now it was time to make the proposal official. Queen Sigrid, in her visit with Gunheid, made the same proposal. Only Signy was told not to mention the purpose of the visit to Wealhtheow because that news should come from her mother or father. But it did not take long for the message to reach the princess. Gunheid soon called her daughter into her modest hall and told her about the arrangement, much to Wealhtheow's joy. When she returned to Signy's side, the news brought squeals of delight from both young women—soon they would be sisters.

With this news, the priestess of Freyja felt some urgency to make an offering to her patron goddess to ensure the health of this royal marriage. It had been Vanadisdottir's vision that Hrothgar was the right husband for Wealhtheow, but it still had to be taken to the goddess Freyja. Since Freyja's father, Njord, lived by and loved the sea and so did Freyja, the water's edge was the right place for such an offering. Things were changing in these times, when the men now worshipped Odin and Thor above all gods. The men took important rituals to high ground, but Vanadisdottir did not want the women to forget the old ways. She asked the two mothers, Wealhtheow and Signy, and the guvernante Fiona to meet her at the bastu at sunrise the next morning. It would be a time for cleansing in preparation for making an offering to Freyja. The sauna was next to a spring-fed pool near the top of the ravine where the three women of Olaf's court had made an offering upon the death of Olfdene the summer before. There, all six women sat together in the sauna, with Vanadisdottir recalling the origin of this ritual.

"One time Njord took Freyja under the sea to watch and to learn from the fish the meaning of the strength of the breath of a fish. But Freyja made other journeys to the bottom of the sea. One day while Freyja was watching several mermaids sunning themselves on the shore, a thought occurred to her that she had never heard anyone speak of an old mermaid. Mermaids never grew old. This was a new realization, and she wanted to learn their secret of youth. Thus she dove down into her father's realm to learn this secret. The beautiful mermaids she watched down there were all in their prime of youth. None showed any signs of aging. She watched them swim to the bottom of the sea and then turn and shoot up to the surface. They were beautiful to watch. She saw them leaving the water to sun themselves on the beaches of the coast. It took Freyja several days of observing them before she found what she was looking for. She had to do some wandering along the bottom of the sea before she found the mermaids doing something that she did not expect. They were up near the shoreline in a deep inlet or fjord along the coast in a place that was boggy. There they were taking the mud of the bog and patting it on their bodies until they were covered from head to fin with mud. They then lay in the sun to allow the mud to dry before they would again dive into the water to wash it off. From that day on, Freyja would come to this boggy place and take a mud bath. This mud is what kept her young. This is why many women stop to cake themselves with mud when they find such a boggy place, and why bogs are a place to throw offerings to Freyja.

"There was once a time when families would place their dead loved ones in hollowed-out logs and throw those logs into a bog. At first they thought this might make the dead person young and healthy again. When they didn't come back to life, they thought that it might not work in just any bog but could happen in the special bog discovered by Freyja, so the search has continued even up till today for that special mud. Then the people grew to believe that maybe it did work, just that the dead person came back as a mermaid. Anyway, it is this story of Freyja's way of keeping young that make bogs sacred places of worship, and sacred places for a maiden to begin her journey into womanhood. That is why we are here today. Wealhtheow is about to begin this journey. We are calling on the gods and goddesses, especially Moðir and her son and grand-daughter, Njord and Freyja, to bless Wealhtheow as she begins this journey. We will soon take her down to the bog and cake her with mud, just as Freyja did. But first we need to cleanse ourselves in this sauna."

The women sat in the sauna for three rounds; after each round in the sauna they plunged into the cool pool of water that formed by the spring near the top of the ravine. The priestess asked that one of the other women present participate in the rest of the ritual with Wealhtheow, to show support, and she suggested that this person be Signy, since Signy felt so close to her soon-to-be sister. The two young women were then led down the ravine, where they were to step out into the bog. There, the two mothers and the two guvernantes covered the two maidens with mud. They then lay in the sun while the mud dried, in this way sealing their bodies in youth in a ritual that honored Freyja by using the seaside mud of Njord. While the two young women were drying in the sun, the priestess returned to the sauna to retrieve the pendant of Idunn that Wealhtheow always wore and so much loved. Upon returning to the young women baking in the sun, she explained to Wealhtheow that because of her love of Idunn, the pendant would be a rightful sacrifice and offering to make to Freyja. Once the mud dried, Wealhtheow took the pendant from Vanadisdottir, held it to her breast one last time, and then threw it out into the bog.

The two girls danced around laughing as the now-dry mud they wore cracked and fell off their bodies in pieces. They then returned to the pool next to the sauna to wash off the remaining dried mud. There, Gunheid had placed a clean, new dress for her daughter to wear, and the old one was thrown into the sauna fire.

Finally, Vanadisdottir instructed the two young women to stand in the Freyja Initiation posture while they moved their attention to their center of harmony.

The Freyja Initiation Posture*

Stand with your feet hip-width apart and your arms crossed below your belly, right arm above the left arm, with the hand of the right hand clasping the left forearm. Your arms may be holding your pregnant belly.

---

*This posture is new and has been determined to be an initiation posture. The figurine was found in Aska, Östergötland, Sweden, and dates from the Viking period.

As they stood in this posture, Vanadisdottir beat her drum rapidly while Wealhtheow and Signy went into an ecstatic trance. Wealhtheow was the first to see the goddess in her cart being pulled by her two cats, two very large cats, but then she saw Signy become one of the cats and felt the strength of the cat as she lay in her den waiting for her he-cat to return. He soon strolled into the den, looking very majestic. He lay down beside her and she started licking his coat, feeling very contented and safe with him. When he again left the den she felt very alone, but then she went out of the den to be with the other female animals of the forest, who were all looking to her for some sort of advice. She felt a great responsibility to them but at the same time felt strong in her ability to fulfill whatever it was they were expecting of her. She looked up and saw the king of the beasts standing not too far away, as another lion approached him. She went to his side to welcome this guest to their forest domain. The message she receives from Freyja's cats is that because of Hrothgar's responsibilities, there will be times when she will be alone, and during those times she will need to be strong for the other women in the domain.

Thus Wealhtheow dedicated her engagement to Hrothgar to the goddess of the Vanir, Freyja. This was the first step in her new life as an adult of the clan. As they returned to Gunheid's hall for breakfast, Fiona related a similar engagement ritual that was made to the goddess Gefjon, another goddess of the Vanir.

Throughout that day Healfdene and Olaf conferred on a number of issues affecting both of them. An important topic was the matter of protecting the land and patrolling the strait between Zealand and Scania. The other matter foremost on their minds was the upcoming marriage that would unite their two families. They decided that the wedding should be that fall, specifically, at the time of the fall equinox. Healfdene felt that it would be useful to their alliance and to the protection of the land for Hrothgar to reside in Scania with Olaf, so that he could help strengthen his defenses against raiders. With Hrothgar living at Olaf's settlement, Halga, Healfdene's youngest son, could prove himself as a warrior and have a chance to learn and demonstrate his skills in leading men.

As for protecting the strait, King Healfdene had yet not decided on the location of the new harbor settlement along the strait. The problem was that across the strait from Olaf's west harbor the land was too boggy and travel was very difficult. "A much better location would be farther to the north," Healfdene said, "but that would be out of sight of the west harbor. From that place it would take considerably less than half a day for a ship to cross to the other harbor. If on the west side of the strait a sentry was placed south of the east harbor, and also on the east side to the north, at the point of land above the west harbor, then sentry fires could easily be seen from the other side. That way when a fire is lit, the sentry seeing it could set a fire on his side that could be seen by the sentry watching from the harbor, and a ship would be able to set out to cross the strait or intercept the foreign ship passing through the strait." Healfdene drew two parallel lines in the dirt and marked the places along either side of the strait as he talked. "If the harbors were spaced that way, the sentry at the west harbor would first see ships coming from the south, and from the east harbor ships coming from the north. In that way a ship leaving the harbor would have a head start in intercepting ships going through the strait. The revenue collected from the ships passing through the strait would be about equal on each side, since about the same number of ships go north as go south. In this way raiders going through the strait could be stopped and fought off. If the raiders knew our positions and tried to avoid the two harbors by sneaking along the opposite bank, when they tried to cross the strait to avoid the next harbor they would be seen by the sentries in between.

"With the help of your amazing shepherd boy, no raiders should get by. Breca visited us and told us about his visit with you. Thanks to the boy, the Jute is still alive. Stopping raiders would give our men a chance to learn and practice how to fight sea battles. Also, with the harbor farther to the north, it would take a ship a little less time to travel from the harbor at the foot of the fjord to the east harbor. With two land outposts between Hleidargard and the east harbor, it would take about a day for relay riders to travel from one harbor to the other, a little longer than from your settlement to the west harbor."

Healfdene had thought a lot about this plan. Olaf saw its advantage and was quick to accept it. With the plan of securing the realm by controlling the ships that pass through the strait established, and with the date set for Wealhtheow's marriage to Hrothgar set, that night was one of celebration. As was the tradition when there were royal visitors, a hunt was planned for the next day, something enjoyed by the men of both tribes, a bonding experience.

The following morning after the hunt, Healfdene was ready to begin his journey back home, but on the way he wanted to stop at the west harbor settlement to meet the men there and to see the view from the point of land north of the harbor. Olaf suggested that the queen and princess could leave on the ship, and that Healfdene might like to ride across the land to the harbor. Both the ship and the land travelers should arrive there at about the same time. Thus Healfdene was given a horse, and the two leaders left on horseback with six men accompanying them. When they arrived at the harbor that evening they found that the ship had already arrived and that the people were settling in for the night. The queen and princess were offered beds in one of the larger halls, while Healfdene and Olaf found beds to their liking in the main hall of the harbor.

The next morning, Healfdene and Olaf rode along the trail north to the point of land that reached out to the west, toward Denmark. The king pointed northwest, to where the sentry to the south of the east harbor could light a signal fire and it could be seen from the point, and a fire set on the point of land could be seen from the west harbor. The king and Olaf were satisfied that these signal fires would quickly send the message from one harbor to the other if a ship was passing through the strait. The queen, princess, and ship's crew had followed the men up the coast and met them at the point. From there, the royal family then left by ship, traveling north on their way home to Hleidargard. Olaf and his men rode off in the opposite direction to return to their settlement. Everyone was pleased with the outcome of this trip.

11

THE WEDDING

An ancient Nordic wedding involves much tradition and ritual, and the Freyja Initiation posture provides me with details about this ancient rite. Then, sitting in the Freyr Diviner posture, I receive more answers to my questions regarding the nuptials. As well, I see that the carving of runes for a wedding memorial provides another opportunity for Thord to take yet another step in his training in becoming a seiðmaðr . . .

About a week before the fall equinox, a well-bedecked ship arrived in the estuary of Olaf's settlement. Aboard was Queen Sigrid and Princess Signy, who were arriving early to help with the wedding preparations. Among the vessel's crew, offering protection to these royal women, was Prince Halga, Healfdene's youngest son. They brought word that the king and Hrothgar would arrive just before the equinox.

The settlement was abuzz with activity. The men were out hunting for meat for the planned days of feasting. The usual activities of spinning and weaving, tending sheep and cows, and harvesting grains and vegetables from the fields were also in full swing. Sufficient food and bedding was needed for wedding guests, who would start arriving two days before the big day. Bread was baking in the hearth, and new straw was being gathered for bedding. Several of the women were busy sewing the gown the bride would wear. Vanadisdottir, both because she was a priestess of Freyja as well as Wealhtheow's guvernante, was involved with preparations for the wedding ritual, with instructions for everyone, particularly the women.

A small group of women, including the two royal mothers and their daughters, were in a forest glen next to a tarn of black water—this was a place of Freyja where the wedding would take place. Several men were clearing fallen branches and other debris from the area to make room for the guests to witness the exchange of vows. Places for special guests to sit were prepared and the entire area decorated. Tallow candles were made in the hollows of pieces of wood to float on the black water, light to brighten the dim light of the glen and to attract the attention of Freyja.

Vanadisdottir stood on the edge of the tarn and called the women together to tell them the story of the goddess Var:

"This place was selected for the wedding as a place of Freyja, the goddess of love. Her golden tears of mourning for the loss of Odr when he went wandering formed these tarns found all over the land. Another goddess important to this wedding is Var. I am sure you have all heard of her. We will call on Var tomorrow to hear the vows made between prince and princess. Besides hearing vows of marriage, Var also punishes those who do not keep their marriage vows. But you may not know her full story. When I learned this story, it was said that Var is a sister of Njord, though some say that she is a sister to Odin. We know that she came of age when giants roamed the earth, before they settled in Jotunheim, the realm of the giants in Midgard. At that time whenever the giants became tired or when night fell, they would lie down wherever they were in order to sleep. It was Var's parents' generation that built the first halls that we have become accustomed to and in which we now sleep.

"Var met a giant, fell in love with him, and they were married. After they were married he did not stay around, but rather went on wandering as giants have always done. Var had other ideas of how a family should be raised. She wanted to have children who would know and could depend on their father. So she was hurt and disappointed when her husband went wandering. She went to Moðir with her pain and recalled that before Odin settled down with Frigg, he had several other sons with other goddesses or giants. 'These children all seem to have problems,' Var said. 'Thor is so impulsive and always getting into trouble. Tyr always wants to please everybody with his bravery. Only Baldr, the son of Odin and Frigg, seems well-adjusted, sensible, and much loved. Look how badly Freyja has been hurt because of her wandering husband, though her two daughters seem to be doing well. Look at all the mischief that Loki, the son of the giants Farbauti and Laufey, gets himself into, and he does so much wandering—I don't know how his wife Sigyn puts up with him. I think when people get married they should make vows to stay together.'

"Hearing this, it was then that Moðir commissioned Var to be the goddess who listens to marriage vows and punishes those who do not keep them. Some time later, Var happened to be sitting along the river that ran near Vanaheim, with Slœgr, Moðir's husband, and Ullr, Moðir's grandson. They were talking about the virtues of the materials they use in their crafts. Slœgr was espousing the virtues of iron. 'Though it takes a hot fire to work with it, it is so much stronger than wood and lasts longer than wood.' Ullr said, 'Carving in wood is so much more delicate and beautiful. It is easier, and beautiful designs can be cut into it.' He accepted the fact that it would not last forever and would eventually rot. Stone was one material that neither god appreciated. It was Var who added, 'Stone can be carved by chipping away at it with iron tools, but this carving is not as delicate. Some stones are used for tools, such as hammers and points for arrows or spears. Memorials are often cut into stone by stonesmiths. These memorial stones will last forever. Running water will eventually wash away stone, but it will also make it beautifully smooth.'

"As Var was talking about the use of stone, she was thinking about the oaths she expected people to make upon getting married, and that an oath was to last forever, just like stone. It was then that she decided an oath should be sworn on a stone, since stones are lasting, and on special occasions the stone used to swear an oath on could be stood up and carved to remember that particular occasion. And so that is why we use stones for the swearing of oaths.

"I need to go out now and find the right stone for the wedding tomorrow, a stone that will not crumble, which can be moved here, to this glen in the forest."

Then Vanadisdottir left them and went to her herb garden. She knew of a large rock there that was buried in the garden and thought it would be just the right stone. She took a stick and began digging around it. It was the perfect size, though it would take six or eight men to move it. When it was uncovered enough for the men to get their hands and ropes around it, she called to Prince Halga to bring the men of his crew to move the stone to the glen. There they dug a hole in which it would stand on its end.

The priestess next had a job for Thord. She knew the power of the runes, the power found in their ability to remember occasions like this wedding. Runes were something that all priests and priestesses needed to know. Runes told the stories of battles and of deaths, as well as marriages and births, stories that are to be remembered forever. Though Thord had no experience as a stonesmith, she knew he had the vision to carve the appropriate runes for the memorial. She found him on the hillside with his sheep and asked him to come with her. She found a charred piece of wood that she could use to sketch the outline of a design of two intertwining serpents winding their way around the stone. She explained that the runes telling of the marriage between Hrothgar and Wealhtheow would be laid out along the back of the snakelike lines she sketched with the charcoal. After the wedding would be the right time to teach Thord the power of the runes. She then sent him off to the blacksmith to get a hammer and chisel with which he would later carve the appropriate runes into the stone after the wedding ritual. Meanwhile, he would carve the snakelike lines into the stone.

That day and the day before, a number of ships had arrived from Denmark, including the one carrying King Healfdene and Prince Hrothgar. Just as on market day when crowds of people camped in the fields around the great hall, campsites could be seen in the fields as far as the edge of the distant woods, with smoke rising from all the individual fires. The kings, chieftains, and princes, along with their warriors, were given places in the great hall to sleep, while the important women were offered places in the halls of the women of equal rank that stood around the great hall. Many of the guests were kinfolk—cousins, uncles, and aunts. A wedding was one of those times when extended family and friends came together to renew their bonds of kinship and friendship. Those who found success in their position in life brought gifts for others to demonstrate their position. These were great times for the exchange of gifts.

Thord was happy for the important job he had been given by Vanadisdottir. He would have felt out of place in the great hall, as his disfigured appearance would have caused people to shun him. That night he built a fire in the wooded glen where the wedding would take place, and there he chipped away at the wedding stone. It was almost dawn when he lay down near a fire to sleep, having completed his carving of the intertwining serpents on the stone. Though this was the first time he had used a hammer and chisel on stone, it did not take him long to discover for himself the best techniques for making the flowing lines that curved back and forth along the wedding monument. It is the respect for the strength of this serpent that surrounds Earth, called Jormungand, that adds to the power and magic of a monument. How could someone read the runes that will eventually flow along its back and not feel its power? How could anyone dare to break a vow made on this stone? Thord was already experiencing the power of the runes.

The next day everyone walked beyond the campsites to find their way to the wooded glen and to stand before this stone monument.

Vanadisdottir found Thord standing at the edge of the glen watching the people arrive. She asked him to fetch his drum; while she was reciting the marriage vows he was to beat his drum to the rhythm of the vows in order to assist the words in entering the cleansed minds of everyone present. In drumming, he was to stand off to one side near the trees. It was the priestess who called to the bride and groom to come forward to stand next to the stone monument, with each placing their left foot on the stone as she led them in the wedding ceremony. Then each of them in turn called the name of Var to listen while speaking the vow of fidelity, protection, love, and care of the marriage partner. Thus it was before this stone and all these people that Hrothgar and Wealhtheow were married.

At the end of the ritual the crowd shouted "Hil! Var!, Hil! Freyja!" and for the sake of the Danes among them, "Hil! Gefjon!" Vanadisdottir caught the one eye of Thord and a smile flowed between them.

A procession led by the bride and groom found its way back to the great hall for an afternoon and evening of feasting, drinking, and merriment. The seats had been arranged for King Healfdene and Queen Sigrid to sit in the elevated position at the end of the hall next to Olaf and Gunheid. Hrothgar and Wealhtheow sat next to them, with Hrothgar a step up from Olaf's chief retainer, Hailgesson. Hrothgar would now take Hailgesson's place in leading Olaf's warriors, a potentially sensitive issue. It was up to Hrothgar to resolve this by becoming friends with and showing respect to Hailgesson. Hrothgar did not know Olaf's men and had the wisdom to ask this champion to continue leading them in their practice and competitions until such time as the prince was able to prove himself as a strong and fair leader. This was on Hrothgar's mind as he sat next to Hailgesson, but it was also an evening of celebration that he knew would end with him joining Wealhtheow in her bed for the first time.

This would mark the first night that Vanadisdottir would not sleep in a room adjacent to Wealhtheow. She did have a place in the hall of the other women, but before she retired for the evening she walked up the hill to the wooded glen where the wedding had taken place, to find Thord camping by the fire next to the stone. She had watched him during the ritual and had seen him leave early. She knew he felt he just didn't fit in with this group of warriors and champions. And she knew it was time to start teaching him the runes. She sat down next to him and began:

"In Odin's pursuit of wisdom he hung on the windswept tree for nine nights, and it was while he hung on that tree that he mastered the mighty magic of the runes. This is your night to begin mastering this magic.

"The first rune, ᚠ, Fehu, is the one who helps in sorrow and sickness, but I think tonight you will not learn the runes in the order that Odin learned them, but rather in the order of inscribing this stone. So let's begin. The stone starts with 'Hrothgar and Wealhtheow were married.' I will show you the runes for that. We begin with the rune Hagalaz, the ninth rune. It is the wrath of nature. It can calm storms to save ships at sea. It can calm the winds. Listen when you speak the name Hrothgar. Hear that first sound in his name. It is that very first sound, and it looks like this." She then drew two parallel lines in the dirt and a line connecting the line near the middle but sloping down to the right, ᚺ. "That is Hagalaz.

"Now listen to the next sound. As you say it, air leaves your open lips, but your lips become more rounded. That sound is Raidho. It is the speed of the arrow traveling through the air. You can see it move but you can't catch it. It looks like this: ᚱ." She then drew a vertical line with two intersecting lines projecting to the right, one from the top angling down, the other at the midpoint angling up, with both lines meeting at a point on the right. Then from the intersection of the line at the midpoint she drew a line angling down and out to the right.

Vanadisdottir continued in this matter with each rune, next

showing Thord the sound of Othala, ᛟ, then Thurlsaz, ᚦ, and then Gebo, ᚷ. When she drew Gebo it was two slanted lines crossing in the middle. The last two marks to make the name Hrothgar were Ansuz, ᚠ and again Raidho, ᚱ. With a burnt stick she began at the head of the serpent that Thord had carved on the stone and drew these marks between the two lines, one after another, speaking the sounds out loud as she drew them.

Thord then pointed to them: ᚺᚱᛟᚦᚷᚠᚱ speaking the sound of H R O TH G A R. A look of amazement came over his face as he spoke the name again. He could see and hear the mighty magic in those marks.

Vanadisdottir then left to return to the hall of the women, while Thord began to carve into the stone those marks that she had made with charcoal. Othala, ᛟ and Kenaz, ᚲ, the two runes that meant *and*, would come next before he would spell out the runes for Wealhtheow, ᚹᛖᚨᛚᚦᛖᛟᚹ. In this way he learned twelve of a total of twenty-three runes that he would eventually learn, to complete this memorial stone of the marriage of Hrothgar and Wealhtheow.

Several days after the wedding, while Healfdene and Sigrid were preparing to return home, Vanadisdottir, with Thord at her side, asked the two royal families to come up to the wooded glen to see the finished stone. She had taken some red clay to fill in the carved symbols so that the design could be better seen. There, Thord told all gathered the meaning of the carving. He pointed to each mark and spoke the sound of each, and as he did, the words flowed from his lips:

"Hrothgar and Wealtheow are married. Hrothgar Healfdeneson and Wealhtheow Olfdottir will rule fairly the Skjǫldung and find wealth and happiness in their life together. The people will feel protected and will honor this future king and queen. The words on this stone will be spoken forever."

Except for Vanadisdottir, those gathered could not appreciate these words as much as Thord did, because he could hear the stone speaking. But the others did understand the meaning of the runes, and with this carving Thord earned from Hrothgar his second armband.

12

THE NIGHTWALKER

Thord is emerging as an important character in this narrative, and now that his behind-the-scenes role in the royal wedding has been revealed, I question how this young man, so different from the others in Olaf's domain, fits in and is able to cope with the prevailing warrior culture. As I ask this question, Thord's story flows forth, showing that he is brought to a new place of acceptance in life. Also, the arrival of Gudvi brings similar questions as to how she will cope with the loss of her family and coming to this settlement in Scania. The narrative unfolds as my questions are answered while sitting in the Freyr Diviner posture . . .

It would probably rain tonight, Thord observed. After he returned the sheep to their pen he walked down to Olaf's hall. He noticed the smoke pouring out of the smoke holes at the two ends of the hall and falling to the ground. The air was heavy. When he entered the hall he found a table at which to sit with several of Olaf's men, and there he felt as heavy as the air, yet he needed to make his appearance in the great hall as was expected of him.

He took a bone of lamb and sat at a table picking at the meat while two of the warriors laughed as they argued, "Your ax is too heavy for you. You could barely swing it."

"What do you mean? You have the marks to prove you are wrong, with that cut on your head. You need to keep your eyes open when trees fall."

Thord looked around. The men at the other tables, swigging down horns of mead, were also playfully combative, arguing about their swords, fighting, and wrestling. Thord felt out of place here. He was not a warrior. The warriors tolerated him, appreciated him for his dreaming skills, even honored him at times, but tonight they were enjoying themselves with their competitive attitudes and their copious drinking. Olaf sat in his high seat playing the role of king, laughing along with his men. Hrothgar sat just below him and praised certain of the men and challenged others whom he thought could do better. All were flexing with the sinew of the bear, being typical berserkers.

Thord soon became bored with their boasting, and got up and walked out of the hall without anyone noticing his departure. He went up the knoll to his hut that he had built for protection from the elements while watching the sheep. It would keep him dry from the rain that was just starting and it was not as smoky in here. His dog, Heim, followed at his heels. Thord spent a few minutes starting a fire just outside of the hut because it was fall and the evenings were becoming cooler. There he sat under the hut's overhang, deep in thought. He was irritated. He felt different from the others here.

From one of the outbuildings in the settlement Vanadisdottir spotted the light of Thord's fire. The priestess bowed out of the womens' quarters, where Wealhtheow was having a conversation with the other women of the settlement, and started up the knoll to be with Thord. She knew that when he sat alone by the fire, this meant he was brooding—and therefore was open to learning.

Thord smiled as she sat down across the fire from him. "Tell me again about the sinew of the bear and the other five strengths," he said.

"I know Olaf's men care only for the sinew of the bear. The story you have so often heard is how Odin tied Fenrir the Wolf in the magical binding made by the dwarfs of the cave of the dark elves. They made the binding with the sound a cat makes when it walks, the sinew of a bear, the roots of a mountain, the spittle of a bird, the breath of a fish, and the beard of a woman. It was the goddesses and gods of the Vanir who discovered these strengths and gave them to the dwarfs. It was Freyja who learned most about the sound a cat makes when it walks—she learned it from her cats as they pulled her chariot. She had often watched her cats stalking without a sound, so silently that even Heimdall, who could hear the grass grow, could not hear them. She was the goddess who most valued the power of stalking, the power of observing the world without being observed, without distraction.

"It was Njord who discovered the power of the breath of a fish and taught it to Freyja by having her watch fish from his domain at the edge of the sea. He had her spend time sitting on the bottom of the sea, watching the fish. She saw the bubbles rising from the grasses where the fish swam, rising to the surface, twisting, turning, and flowing around any obstacle that might get in the way. She saw the power of flowing like a bubble, letting any attack on her flow by, like water off her back.

"It was Freyr, in watching a warrior with a short sword fight by stepping in so close to his opponent that his opponent had no room to swing his sword, who learned of the power of the spittle of a bird. He was searching for the best way to describe this warrior's style of fighting, of sticking to his opponent like glue, when he discovered the strength of the glue formed from the spittle of a swallow making a mud nest in the eave of his hall. Mud made just from water becomes crumbly when it dries, but the mud of a swallow's nest is hard and does not crumble.

"It was Njord who learned to value the roots of a mountain. He, like his son, spent some time watching Odin's warriors fighting. He very much valued the center of harmony, the place just a few centimeters below the umbilicus. In watching the men fighting he was sensitive to noticing the way their center of harmony dropped when they planted themselves in such a way that they could not be moved. It was this power of the trees in being rooted that protected the Vanir in their battle with the Æsir. With his love for the trees he did not want to liken this strength of the warrior to that of a tree. He believed that all this fighting was foolish. From his explorations of caves deep in the sea he knew that mountains rested on deep roots of rock. With this knowledge, it was Njord who named this strength the power of the roots of a mountain.

"Though all of the Vanir value the strength of the beard of the woman, it was Skaði, the wife of Njord, who has taught us about this strength. During the famous feast given by Ægir to show off his new ale cauldron, Loki proceeded to insult each god and goddess. He thought he had gotten in the last word in his harangue of Skaði with the retort, 'When you beckoned me to your bed, your words were so much sweeter then.' He did not hear Skaði's priceless retort: 'Even with the hairs growing from my chin you found me attractive. At my age I am happy with all that I can get. Everyone should cheer me for it. I know that Njord cheers me. He is proud of me.' These words show the strength of the beard of a woman.

"Of all of these strengths, I believe the strongest and most magical is the sound a cat makes when it walks. The power of the cat and the power of dreaming are the two greatest powers of magic. Tonight when you left Olaf's hall to sit by the fire to think, you became a stalking cat. The sinew of a bear is blind, and because it is blind warriors get in trouble, like Thor, whose blind temper got him in trouble when he competed with the giant Utgard-Loki and lost. Once you are centered in your place of harmony, stalking what is going on around you is a much more powerful strength. Did you notice the two wood-cutting warriors? One had a cut above his eye. I had to treat his wound this afternoon after a tree fell and a branch hit him on the head. He was chopping with the sinew of a bear, racing against his friend, but not with the stalking of a cat.

"By sitting on this hillside with your sheep and at night by this fire, you have cultivated quietness and have learned the patience of stalking and dreaming. The sinew of a bear only interferes with what you can learn while you are stalking and dreaming. Valuing and living these two magical strengths is the most important lesson of becoming a seiðmaðr."

Vanadisdottir left Thord with these thoughts as she returned to the women's hall.

Thord spent the night in his small hut. He felt the peace of the night, something he had not felt much since he had left his family's farmstead. He found peace in the quiet of the hills and the smell of the night air. Sleeping inside Olaf's great hall disrupted his peace; it was noisy in there at night, with the sounds of the warriors' snoring and their other body noises. The great hall also had a foul smell. Thord took comfort in the sounds of the night, of the owls and other night animals. The sound of the stream running down to the shore and the water lapping on the distant shoreline was soothing. This was where he belonged.

Though he spent some time in the great hall and would sometimes eat with the warriors of the settlement, he would usually leave to return to his hut on the hillside. Even the food eaten by the king's retainers did not always agree with him, so he often would cook for himself using the plants and herbs he gathered himself. He was beginning to learn about the power of plants and wanted to experiment with them. The men of the hall, after spending an evening drinking, would leave the hall to relieve themselves and see Thord's fire on the hillside. Sometimes Thord would be sitting beside it or sometimes he would be wandering the hillsides in the night. He soon became known to these warriors as Nöttgangr, or Nightwalker. His night vision was almost as good as that of most night animals, just like Vanadisdottir, who could also see in the night. He valued nighttime as being the time for dreaming and stalking around Olaf's settlement, learning from the sounds and habits of the animals of the night. These animals told him a lot, and Heim was always at his side during these excursions.

One night as they walked together, with Heim trotting some distance ahead of Thord, the dog turned and came running back whimpering. He turned to run ahead a couple of times, telling Thord to hurry because he had found something. As they came to the shallow ravine that ran down to the shore, the same ravine on which Vanadisdottir had built her bastu, he heard the sound of a child crying. When he opened the door to the bastu, he found a young girl, eight or nine years old, cowering in the corner. Heim trotted over to her and nuzzled her gently, showing the girl gentle canine affection. With that reassurance, the girl was quick to put her arm around the dog's furry neck. The girl's face was streaked with tears. In the darkness she could not see Thord's disfigured face; instead, his soft voice and gentle manner helped quiet her, and he led the girl back to his hut. She told him of raiders from the sea who had attacked her family's farm, killed the other members of her family, and burned down the farm. Her older brother had run with her into the woods and hid her in a hollow log before he had been caught. From her hiding place she saw one of the raiders cut off her brother's head and fling it across the clearing before taking from his neck the leather thong that held a simple carving of Mjollnir, Thor's hammer. From her hiding place the girl had heard this barbarian shout to another, "Someone who died without fighting does not deserve to wear Mjollnir." Gudvi—for that was her name, she told Thord—had then wandered westward along the coast for three days, and on this, her third night, she finally found shelter.

Thord sent Heim to fetch Vanadisdottir. By the time the priestess arrived, Thord had washed Gudvi's face and the girl sat by the fire with a bowl of warm broth in her hands. Weather permitting, Thord preferred to sit outside the hut, by the firepit he had built there, but on this night they sat together around a new fire pit inside his hut that had an air channel running from the rocks in the bottom of the pit to the outside of the hut for air to fuel the fire.

Thord heard Gudvi's story again as she told it to the priestess, and his outrage grew upon this second hearing. He grabbed the Mjollnir he also wore and tore it from his neck, exclaiming, "How can I be wearing this if that is what it means?" Even though all the warriors of the settlement wore the hammer of Thor in this way, Thord threw his into the fire, to the shock of Gudvi, who knew that all men wore one. Vanadisdottir put her arm around Thord's shoulder to reassure him, as he protested, "And my name too—how can I carry the name of Thor as my name?"

Vanadisdottir suggested, "Maybe it is time we give you a new name, your seiðmaðr name." Though he was still learning, he had learned much more in his first year of training than Vanadisdottir had in hers; it was at the end of her first year at the shrine of Freyja that each of the novices had been given a new name, their priestess name. That was when she had been given the name Vanadisdottir. Telling Thord this, the priestess said, "This seems to be the right time for you take a new name, and I believe the name I have been thinking of is the right name for you. Over the next few days we need to prepare you for your new name. We will start tomorrow, but now I think I need to take Gudvi down to Wealhtheow's hall so that the other women can welcome her here." With that, the priestess left with the little girl.

Word of the arrival of Gudvi quickly reached Gunheid, and from her the news went straight to Olaf. When Olaf learned of the new girl who had come to the settlement in the night he decided that she should be placed in the care of Vanadisdottir, at least for the next few days.

The next morning Olaf went to see Gudvi and found the girl sick, lying in the hall of the women on Vanadisdottir's sleeping platform. She was having difficulty breathing—her lungs were all congested. She had spent two nights alone in the woods, cold, and without sleep. This is when Olaf officially put her in the care of the priestess. Vanadisdottir had made her a broth from *alant,* or elecampane, *kongelys,* or mullein, *følfod,* or coltsfoot, and balsam. Each of these herbs helped relieve lung congestion. Thord remained nearby, concerned for Gudvi. He left to get his drum and returned to drum for the priestess, as he could hear her quietly speaking the words of "Plants of the Mother." Gudvi watched with big eyes as Vanadisdottir brewed this medicinal broth in a kettle over the fire, stirring it with a wooden spoon. Over the next few days Gudvi's breathing improved, and as she felt stronger she began to ask many questions. After she was up and around, everyone in the settlement knew where she could be found—in the shadow of the priestess.

As for the preparations for Thord receiving his new name, Vanadisdottir had spent several hours each day over a period of three days with Thord. The first part of preparing him was to review what he had learned since recovering the ram from the outlaws up north. First, he had learned the power of moving his attention to his center of harmony. From that center he knew he could journey to see what was happening in other places, beyond ordinary vision. He learned that from his center of harmony he could see what others could not see. He was becoming effective in using this power and had the sense to know that with practice, patience, and curiosity there was much more he could use it for. Vanadisdottir knew that he was better in using its power than she had been after her first year as a novice.

The second power he had learned was to pay attention to his dreams, and by paying attention to his dreams he was able to dream more vividly. In paying attention to his dreams, again with a sense of patience, gentleness, and curiosity, he discovered that he could see and sense what others could not see and sense. He could see into the future, and he could see distant places. He had discovered this power by himself, in contrast to Vanadisdottir, who had learned this power from her teachers. To make such discoveries he had learned to use the power of the sound a cat makes when it walks, which is the power of stalking.

In bringing all these powers together, Thord was not just able to see into the future or see distance places, he could also see at night. He was beginning to see inside of other people, as well—what Vanadisdottir called *intuition*. And he was beginning to see inside animals and even plants. The priestess had instructed him to hold those plants about which he might be curious against his center of harmony and dream about them. In this way he could learn the power of plants. He had used this technique infrequently, but he was aware of its usefulness. Vanadisdottir had also told him about the powers of the sinew of a bear, the roots of a mountain, the spittle of a bird, the breath of a fish, and the beard of a woman. He knew these stories and knew that these strengths were available to him, though he had not yet felt an urgency to perfect them. He had also learned the runes and how to read and write them, and the power of poetic words, especially when spoken to the beat of a drum.

When the priestess quizzed Thord about these powers of magic, she appreciated his depth of understanding in such a short time. It was apparent to her that he was a natural seiðmaðr. The early injuries to his face and his resulting blindness in one eye had caused him to leave behind the usual understanding of the power of the sinew of a bear, the power that was the focus of interest for most young boys. This had opened him to learning other, greater powers. He was ready to take a new name, to leave behind the name Thord, a name that belonged to the sinew of a bear, and take a name that would describe the greater powers that he had learned. And Vanadisdottir knew just the name for him.

The next step was to create an appropriate naming ceremony. What would be most appropriate would be for this ceremony to be performed among men for this special young man, but there were no men around them who could appreciate these powers of magic and therefore the new name that was to be given to Thord. Though his father would not understand, his father would likely be supportive and would appreciate that his son had found a place in life that he valued. Also, Dan, the boy who had taken Thord's place when he left his family, had experienced the magical powers of Thord. Olaf had experienced his power, too, and was open-minded enough to give Thord his support. Vanadisdottir hoped that these three would be a sufficient number of males for the ceremony. Since she was performing the ritual—a very unusual position for a woman—she felt that both Wealhtheow and Gudvi would be supportive, and Wealhtheow, Gunheid, and Hrothgar should also be part of the ceremony.

Thus, the priestess asked for an audience with Olaf to explain to him the purpose of this ceremony and to ask for his support. In gaining his support she asked if he would send a couple of his retainers north, to ask Dan and Thord's father to come to the settlement. Thord mentioned that he would like his cousin to come too. Olaf agreed to send for these three.

The day the three arrived at the settlement, Vanadisdottir met with them to tell them the reason why they had been summoned. They, like Olaf, did not have a deep understanding about the significance of the ceremony and Thord's name change. At first his father was a little hurt that he wanted to change his name, a name he had given him in pride, but for Thord's sake, because it was obviously important to him and his new position as a novice seiðmaðr, his father agreed to lend his support. People were both afraid of and awed by a seiðmaðr. Very few people had ever met a seiðmaðr and the idea scared his father a little, but what else could a boy do in life, half blind and disfigured as his son was? He was greatly disappointed when his son was injured, knowing that he would never become a warrior. He was pleased to hear from the priestess about how Thord had excelled in learning the magic of a seiðmaðr, and was even impressed by some of the stories he had heard. In the end, he felt he had to support his son in this venture.

The next evening the naming ceremony began with a cleansing sauna for the men—Thord, Olaf, Hrothgar, Thord's father, his cousin, and Dan. Thord had been instructed to tell the other men of his experiences of magical power. Vanadisdottir had made him a new tunic, which he put on after the cleansing sauna. Once the men returned from the sauna to the fire blazing in the clearing on the hill, near the stone where Hrothgar and Wealhtheow were married, they all sat down to hear the words of the priestess. She beat the drum to cleanse and open the minds of all those present as she spoke:

"Most of you grew up hearing the stories of the Æsir, the stories of great warriors who value the strength of Odin, his son Thor, and the other warrior gods. But even these stories point to another son of Odin as the most beloved of the gods—the gentle Baldr. At the end of time it is Baldr who will survive and bring us into the New Dawn, Nydagan, the new world of peace and compassion. Baldr knows a different strength, a strength more powerful than the warrior's strength of the sinew of the bear. Baldr has learned the strength of magic. It is this strength that your young shepherd, your son, your cousin has learned. Each of you has experienced in some way some of his magic. It is his blindness and disfigurement that prevents him from using the sinew of a bear and has led him to discover the more ancient powers of the Vanir—the powers learned by Baldr. Baldr married one of the Vanir, a granddaughter of Moðir. He married Nanna, a cousin of Freyja, and they had a son, Forseti. Forseti was brought up with both the Vanir and the Æsir. He learned the power of compassion and became the compassionate judge in resolving conflict, the only god who was able to silence the cutting tongue of Loki.

"As they sat in Idunn's garden together, Forseti showed Loki that they thought a lot alike. They both saw the foolishness of constant fighting. They both saw that fighting only destroyed, and in the end resolved nothing. They both saw the hypocrisy of the gods in their love of fighting and their love for the gentle Baldr. But it was Loki who confronted the gods with his sharp tongue and tricks, tricks that demonstrated their hypocrisy, tricks like setting up the death of Baldr. It was Baldr's son, though, who showed Loki that compassion and understanding was stronger than his pointed tongue, and in the end it was Baldr who would live to bring peace to the world. As the two gods sat in Idunn's garden, it was Loki who became silent.

"I now offer you a new son of Forseti." Vanadisdottir held out her hand, beckoning Thord—hereafter to be called Forsetason—to come to her side. She turned to those assembled men. "Forsetason may make you uncomfortable because he is different from you. He does not wear the Mjollnir. But you have already come to value his knowledge and judgment, each of you in your own way. Open yourselves up to his knowledge and skill and you will find a greater power in the effectiveness of your leadership."

Then, turning to address Hrothgar specifically, she said, "For those of you of the Skjǫldung, you look to Gefjon, a goddess of the Vanir, as your ancestor. As descendents of Gefjon you have experienced the compassionate power of the kings before you. It is this compassion, balanced with the sinew of a bear, that made these kings great. The retainers of these kings may not have valued this quality of compassion, but the kings knew better. It is Forsetason who will be there to remind you of the magic of compassion."

The men then left to return to Olaf's great hall, and the women to their halls. Forsetason was left alone with Vanadisdottir to meditate by his fire. She had another lesson for him. She showed him how to stand in the posture of the Nyborg Man.*

Vanadisdottir then began to rapidly beat her drum, as Forsetason stood in ecstatic trance. When she finished drumming he reported his experience to her. He was in the hall with the warriors, feeling very uncomfortable, feeling like he did not belong there. As he walked through the hall among the warriors who were talking with one another, they would turn their backs to him as he walked by. So he left and went up the hill, not to his hut, but to a cave, a cave of Moðir, where he sat until the sun came up. He then left and went down to his hut and sat, somehow feeling very different. He reported that he did not feel irritated with the warriors, even though he thought their drunken behavior was foolish. He felt strong in his own way, confident. He then again went into the hall. He saw the warriors drinking and no longer felt like the unaccepted boy, but that he knew something they did not know, and he felt good about himself. He felt that if a warrior approached him and was open to him, he would have something to show him or teach him, but he had another purpose in mind for being in the hall. He walked up to Olaf because there was something he wanted to tell the king, something about a dream that he had had, and he felt the other men turn to watch him as he approached the high seat. Olaf beckoned him to come into his private chambers, where they could talk. His message to Olaf had something to do with a dream about Gefjon being on his side. Then the drumming ended.

---

*This initiation posture was found in an artifact in Nyborg, Fyn, Denmark; thus it is known as the Nyborg Man posture, and is also known as the Feathered Serpent posture in Belinda Gore's works. You can find more on this posture in Gore's *Ecstatic Body Postures,* 218–23.

The Nyborg Man Posture

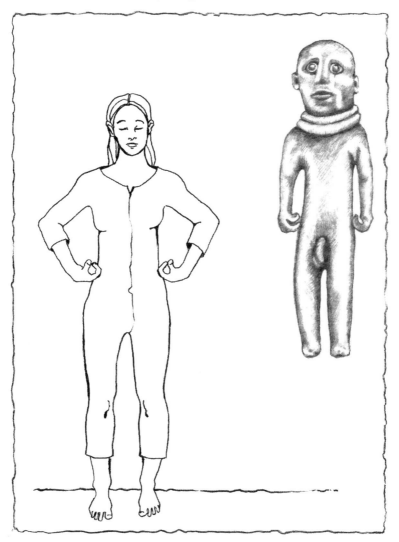

Stand with your feet parallel, about six inches apart, knees slightly bent, with toes pointing straight ahead. Cup your hands and place them at your sides at waist level with fingers pointing up and thumbs pointing forward, with your arms rounded outward and elbows pointing to either side. Face straight ahead with your eyes closed and your mouth slightly open.

Later that evening, Hrothgar retired to the hall of his wife and lay beside her in her bed. He was silent at first, but the princess knew he was troubled. Finally, he spoke: "I am afraid that we have offended Thor and that he will turn against us." As the leader of the warriors his fear was a valid concern, and he was looking for reassurance from Wealhtheow.

She answered, "Forseti is a loved and respected god too. He is the nephew of Thor, and though they may not always agree, Thor knows there is a place for him among the gods. I expect that Thor believes that Forseti, not being a warrior, will end up with Hel, the daughter of Loki and Angrboda, whom Odin threw into the underworld to care for those who died, not of honor in battle, but of illness and old age. I do not believe that Forseti will be punished in this way and know that there are other alternatives. Thor will not turn against you for valuing the judgment of his nephew Forseti and a priest of his, Forsetason. Your men may not understand this. They think that if they show belief in anything but power, Thor will diminish their strength. They do not have to turn to Forsetason. But when you become king, you will need to appreciate the power of compassion, as well as the power of the bear."

With these words of his wife, Hrothgar became quiet and eventually fell asleep.

13

SKALD BRAGASON

Again the story reaches what feels like a hiatus, which leads me to again ask the general question, "What happens next?" The Freyr Diviner posture allows me to see a new turning point for Forsetason with the coming of a skald to Olaf's settlement. The arrival of this poet brings new life and magic to the people . . .

The winter solstice was approaching, only a few weeks away. The settlement was preparing for winter. On this afternoon the dogs started barking and children came running back to the hall shouting that some strange man was walking along the road from the east. When the word passed of who it was that was coming their way, the excitement grew—it was Skald Bragason. He was recognized because of his colorful patched clothing and large floppy hat, the typical costume of a skald. It was rare that a skald would come to the settlement this late in the year. Because of this, everyone knew he was going to stay with them for the winter. No skald had spent the entire winter here for at least five years. What a special winter this was going to be—his presence would make those cold months seem much shorter.

Olaf took his place in his high seat to prepare to greet the skald, while everyone else ran into the hall. Bragason came in, threw his pack against the wall, and as he walked toward Olaf he swept his arm across the front of his body, swinging it toward the floor with a bow, announcing, "Bragason at your service." Everyone was grinning widely, and with this announcement they all cheered. They loved Bragason's entertaining stories.

That evening, Bragason told stories of his travels, especially of his time spent with King Athils. His stories were for entertainment, but more importantly they were also for teaching and healing. In telling his stories he used a drum, but he used it more for calling the attention of his listeners and to accentuate certain parts of his story. Sometimes when monsters or something scary would come into the story, he would beat his drum, making the listeners jump. This evening this poet's stories were for the warriors who sat at the tables in front of their king— stories about battles of winning and losing, battles at sea and on land, battles of protecting one's land and of raiding the land of others. The stories taught battle strategies, but more important to Bragason, they taught values—the value of bravery, the value of commitment, the value of working together with trust, and the value of benevolence. That is where the story of Athils came in.

Athils, the king of Upsala, the king of the Ynglings, was famous for his greed and for intimidating people. His father had been a great and benevolent king and had a superb following. His son, though, had a very different temperament. After his father's death, the goal of the new King Athils was to horde wealth. Because of his inherited power he had a large following—twelve powerful champions and twelve strong berserkers—but their loyalty could not always be trusted. Some would leave when they found other chieftains who showed them more appreciation and benevolence. Athils was very self-centered, a characteristic that would lead to his eventual demise, though his cunning and use of magic kept him in power for many years.

Bragason's stories were about Athils's champions, who would leave and eventually return with some other chieftain to fight against this corrupt king. Yet there were also stories about how the king's cunning, deceptive, dishonorable ways would allow him to win or escape. The crowds listening to Bragason's stories of Athils were quick to hiss at this wicked king, and cry when their heroes would lose to his underhanded tactics. This king seemed to always have a way to escape to save himself. His hall had a number of hidden underground tunnels. He was known for abandoning his men when it appeared that he might lose. For the women in the hall listening to these stories, he would tell of Athils's cruelty to his wives and how his wives did not trust him—again bringing hisses and tears, or cheers, depending on how the story turned. This evening was enjoyable for all, as would be all the evenings of winter.

One of the stories Bragason told was of Athils's seven wives. This king had four children by his oldest wife, three by the next, two by the third wife, and one child by the fourth. It just so happened that five of his children were boys and five girls. The youngest was already five years old, and Athils wanted more children, but as hard as he tried none of his three youngest wives became pregnant. He was an insecure king. Though you might think that his cruelty showed that he was strong, on the contrary, it was evidence of his insecurity. He was afraid that his men would no longer think of him as a man, and this only made him more cruel to his men, and especially to his wives.

After a few years without a royal birth, the wives found a way to make their lives better. The younger wives wanted children, too, and knew it was not going to happen with King Athils. He was getting old and fat. One of the older wives had what others thought were magical powers, and it was she who hatched a plan. Though others thought that the king's ability to escape from harm was a demonstration of Athils' own magical powers, his wives knew about the tunnels he used because several of them ended in their bedchambers. He would use them when he went out prowling for new maidens, in whom he would plant his impotent seed.

The older wives who already had children put up with him because he was the father of their children. He showed them enough respect, and they escaped much of his cruelty because he valued their role as mothers; otherwise he showed little interest in them. One of the older wives, though, felt sorry for the younger childless wives. This older wife with her magical powers knew how to make herself appear much younger, especially in the dark bedchamber, with her touch, voice, and words of seduction. She knew the herbs to use in making ointments to keep her skin silky and tight. Though her hair was turning gray, it didn't appear gray in the dark. She would use herbs to make herself smell younger and beautiful at night, while during the day she would smell old. She was the most slender of the older wives, but during the day she would hide her slender body with dresses to look like the others. The younger wives would share their silken and linen night shifts with her to replace the woolen one she usually wore. When the wives got together they would laugh about how easy it was to deceive the king.

When the king would call for one of his wives and the older wife would go to his bedchamber, the younger wives were free to be with the men they really loved, and as they became pregnant one by one and year by year, their children were treated well by the king, who thought they were all his. The wives' lovers, most all of them important retainers to Athils, knew these children were not the king's, but they kept the secret, knowing it was best for everyone concerned—child, wife, and self.

As the first five boy children of the king grew into adulthood they each practiced the skills to become a warrior as the king had hoped, but none showed the potential to become as great as the king's champions. Athils wanted one of the sons—hopefully the oldest—to be the chief of his warriors and to eventually become king. He believed that this son needed to be as strong as any of his warriors. As it turned out, the king's wish came true with his seventh son. This son was the strongest of all his sons, and as he grew it was apparent that he would soon be able to be the leader of the king's men. Only the present chief of the king's men knew that this young man was in fact his own son, and not the son of the king.

As Bragason told this story, Olaf shouted, "How do you know this, if only the king's champion knows?"

Bragason, with a big smile, answered, "Anyone can see in looking at the boy next to his father that the king could not be his father, but no one in Athils's domain would dare put that to words, and the king so badly wanted a strong son that he would not admit it either."

It was this story that in years to come would give the future King Hrothgar the advantage in battling with Athils. In fact, this champion of King Athils and his son, together with the son's mother, the wife of the king, would eventually come to offer their services to the Skjǫldung king.

The next morning, Bragason, being a skald, needed to commune with the gods by spending time alone in the forest. While wandering through the woods above the settlement, listening to the trees, he found a clearing and a rune stone standing at its edge. He read the stone, for he was well-versed in runes and saw that it was a stone to commemorate the wedding of Hrothgar and Wealhtheow. He was surprised to see the stone. He knew that only special people of wisdom knew the runes. No warriors and not many kings had time for runes. From his earlier trips to this settlement he knew of no one with this wisdom except Vanadisdottir, and she did not have the arm of a carver. Upon returning to the great hall he asked Hrothgar about the stone and who had carved it.

That afternoon, when the men were busy with their chores and games and the women with their spinning and needlework, the skald came up to Forsetason sitting by his hut watching the sheep. He praised him for his carving of the wedding stone. "How important it is to learn the runes. Hil! Odin! for hanging on Yggdrasdill, the World Tree, in search of wisdom. Hil! To the god who gave us the runes. Yet do you know that people knew how to write stories long before Odin gave us the runes? They wrote in pictures. When I was with the Geats and when I was with the Ynglings I saw many picture carvings on the stones in the area, and they told the old stories. I learned many of my stories from reading these stones. The best ones are found in the land of the Geats."

Bragason smiled when he saw how quickly he had gotten Forsetason's attention, for he knew that he had found someone unusually open to learning.

"Who carved those stones?" Forsetason asked.

"You have heard of Ullr, Sif's son and the stepson of Thor, the great craftsman of the Vanir, the god who first made the bow and arrow and the first skis? He carved stories in the wooden pillars of the great hall of the Vanir and in stone. He taught the people how to record stories in stone long before Odin gave us the runes. They say among the Geats that these stones were carved by Ullr, so far back that no one can remember."

"What are in these stories?" the young man inquired.

Bragason could not stop now, he had found a willing student. "If you went to the west harbor and followed the coast north as far as it goes before it turns west, and then south, you will come to Norway and to the land of King Hring. A day or two before you would reach Norway you would have to cross a large river, the Göta River, which runs to the ocean from the great lake Vänern."

"I know about that lake. The goddess Gefjon made that lake when her four sons plowed the earth out to sea to make the island where Hrothgar was born."

Bragason affirmed this with a nod of his head. "The land along this river and up along the lake to Norway is the land of the Geats. They are known as great shipbuilders and fisherman because of this lake and the trees along the lake. The water is quieter than the water of the ocean, and the trees provide plenty of wood, a perfect place for shipbuilding. This place is envied by all. Hreðel, the king of the Geats, is getting old, so his son Hygelac, who will someday be king, protects this land with his warriors, twelve champions, and twelve berserkers. This is a powerful army of men.

"One of the stories found carved in the rocks along this coastline is of an attack on this army, but an attack that happened many, many years ago. It shows many warriors coming from the north, from what is now the land of King Hring, both by land and by sea. I believe they were coming from Norway since they came by land and the ancient king of Norway would not let others cross his land to make this attack.

Jormungand, the great sea serpent, was thrashing his tail because some of the men were thrown overboard on their way by sea, and the carvings show the great worm swimming after one of them. But the Geats are not caught by surprise. You can see their sentry guarding the approach to their land with his long arms outstretched. It is in this place, before the warriors of Norway reached the river, that the battle began. The king or the leader of the king's champions was seen embracing his wife, preparing to leave for the battle. I think it was probably the king because nearby you can see a circular shield wall around the king empty except for the armless king and a one-horned warrior to protect him. Below that you see that the king has fallen and his wife is kneeling next to his head saying good-bye as a ship of death takes him by the right leg to Hel instead of Valhalla because he did not die in battle.

"But this was not the end of the battle. Flying above all of this was Thor in his chariot pulled by a goat. We know that it was flying because of the bird marking in the middle. The warriors from the north reached the Göta River, where the Geats made their stand. Their great warriors held off the warriors from the north to protect their land. One ship was seen crossing the river, but other ships stopped it and the men of the north could go no farther. Someday you'll need to see these rock pictures."

With this, Bragason left to return to Olaf's hall, leaving Forsetason deep in thought.

Often during the day, Bragason would spend time with the women as they spun and wove, while watching the younger children in their games. For the women, he told stories of healing. One story was of a young bully who would torment his younger brother and the other children of the village, for most villages had such a bully and the people would not know what to do about it. In this story he called the bully Eirik.

"When Eirik was only four years old, his mother gave birth to his brother. This infant was sickly and needed constant attention. Eirik was very jealous of all the time his mother gave to his younger brother. When no one was looking he was quick to tease and torment his brother by poking him and taking things from him, making him cry. His parents knew what was going on and whenever they heard their sickly son crying they knew that Eirik was the cause of it and would punish him. As a result, Eirik did not feel loved. He would leave to find other children, but he was not happy and the other children would irritate him. He would then pick on the other children, getting into fights with them and taking their wooden swords or other playthings. Nothing went right for Eirik. None of the other children liked or trusted him, except for one older boy who somehow knew how bad Eirik must have felt, with no friends. This older boy tried to be his friend, but Eirik would become irritated with him, too, and then do something to hurt this friend.

"During the summer I visited that village and met Eirik. He was sitting by himself, looking sad. When I went and sat with him he was not very nice to me either and told me to leave him alone. The women of the village were sitting nearby, spinning and weaving while watching the younger children, just as you are doing now. They did not know what to do, so I went to them and told them a story about another boy, Lokison, who I had met in another village. When Lokison was four years old his baby brother was born, who was sickly, and so his parents had to give all their attention to the new baby and ignored Lokison. When Lokison would get in trouble for tormenting his baby brother he would leave to find other children, but he would quickly become irritated with these other children, fight with them, and take their things. It did not take long for all the other children in the village to avoid him. But as I told the women of that village a story an amazing thing happened. Some of the boys were listening and one of the other boys, a little older than Lokison, went over and sat by Lokison, who was sitting alone looking sad. He just sat with Lokison and said nothing. Soon another boy joined them, and then another as they listened to my story. It was not long before all of the boys of the village were sitting around Lokison, and Lokison began to smile, and as my story came to an end, they all got up and began to play together with Lokison among them, smiling and laughing.

"As I told the women and children of Eirik's village the story of Lokison, an amazing thing happened again. One of the older boys went over and sat by Eirik, soon joined by another, and then another. Soon all of the young boys were sitting around Eirik, and soon Eirik was smiling and laughing with them as they played. Eirik's mother was among the women listening to the story, and that evening she prepared a special meal for Eirik, something she knew he liked, and his father told him a hunting story and told him that when he was a little older he would take him hunting, but first he would make him his own wooden spear that he could use to practice throwing at a tree stump. After that, Eirik was much more pleasant and happy in playing with his younger brother and the other children in the village."

It just so happened that in the settlement of Scania no one could think of a boy like Eirik or Lokison, except for possibly Forsetason. They felt a lot of respect for him because of his special powers. He was not a bully, but his hideous appearance caused some people to avoid him. Yet after that story they tried to give Forsetason more attention and include him in more of their activities. Thus Bragason taught them the magical power of compassion by using the magical power of storytelling.

In listening to these stories told by the skald, the winter went by fast. As spring approached, the talk was of when Bragason would leave and where he would go next. He finally announced that he was going north and expected to spend the next winter among the Geats. With this in mind he asked if he could take Forsetason with him, asking by telling another story:

"When I was last in Norway I met a young man who showed great promise in being a seiðmaðr. He was much like Forsetason. He had been practicing his skills in magic for three years, and I think he knew about as much as Forsetason has already learned. I took him with me to visit the Geats and taught him how to read the stone carvings. He learned these stories and has discovered the magic of storytelling, a power that all seiðmaðr should know."

He told this story to Vanadisdottir and to Olaf, waiting for them to suggest that he take Forsetason with him. Olaf asked, "If Forsetason would go with you, how long would he be gone?" Olaf valued Forsetason's presence in the settlement. Bragason answered that he might be gone for over a year: "If he left this spring to travel with me and he spent the winter among the Geats, he could return by next spring." Bragason showed respect to the king by asking him first rather than leaving the decision up to Forsetason. Vanadisdottir took the proposal to Forsetason, and with her opinion that what he would learn from Bragason would be very valuable, Forsetason decided to go and became excited about the upcoming journey.

14

FORSETASON'S TRAVELS WITH THE SKALD

On his journey with Skald Bragason to the land of the Geats, Forsetason will for the first time hear stories of and actually meet Beowulf, the great Geat warrior and hero. He will also see and learn of the magic of the ancient petroglyphs of Tanum. Many questions arise over the course of a week as I journey in the Freyr Diviner posture, asking about how they travel, what happens on the journey, and what specifically Forsetason learns. Each answer to my question typically leads to another question, as the story continues . . .

In preparation for the journey to the land of the Geats, Skald Bragason asked Vanadisdottir to collect scraps of material of many colors and honor Foresetason with clothing of bright colors, those of a wandering bard. Most important was a large hat that would flop down over the disfigured side of his face so that he would appear more acceptable and not frighten people. With the help of the women of the settlement, it took only a couple of days to finish the multicolored jacket and floppy hat to Bragason's specifications. Forsetason tried them on and all were quick to see that no one at first noticed the ugly scars on his face. Yet Bragason told him that his most worn clothes, clothes that made him look like a poor beggar, would also be useful on such travels, for with that appearance outlaws would leave them alone. Thus, with his needed belongings carefully packed in his knapsack along with a blanket for when they slept along the trail and his drum secured by a strap around his shoulder, Forsetason was ready to go.

They left, first taking the well-worn road to the west harbor and from there up the coast. Inland, the coast was lined with homesteads where the two traveling entertainers were welcomed to stay most every night. Though in earlier generations the people preferred to live on the coast near the water, with the change in beliefs, of venerating Odin and Thor rather than Moðir and Njord, of valuing physical strength and wealth rather than magic and nurturance, most people now thought it safer to live farther inland from the coast, where they were more protected from raiders from the sea. At these farmsteads the travelers were always offered an evening meal and morning breakfast along with sufficient food to carry with them for a satisfying lunch around midday.

Forsetason never tired of hearing Bragason's stories, and as they walked together Forsetason rehearsed telling these stories himself, finding those ways to express them that would excite the emotions of listeners. In time he would be ready to recount them aloud to Bragason for practice and to learn from him the finer points of storytelling. It was obvious that Bragason had much experience as an actor, and one of his skills was the show of emotions in the expressions of his face. This was a major problem for Forsetason because he was able to show those emotions on only one side of his face, but with the other side covered and by exaggerating these expressions on his good side, he was fast learning this skill.

What he needed most was to tell his own story—the story of how he was injured, a story that would explain his odd appearance. The story would tell of how as a young boy he had intercepted several outlaws who were raiding his family's steading. With one swing of the outlaw's sword, across the left side of his face, he had lost his ear, was blinded in one eye, and suffered a severe gash that had left him disfigured on that side of his face. It just so happened that when this occurred Vanadisdottir was nearby and was called on to tend to his wounds. As a result of Vanadisdottir's healing, he survived, though he was severely scarred for life. In telling his own story in the right way, the emotions of others would flow from fear to awe and wonder. So he began a new journey learning the magic of storytelling.

Forsetason was soon ready to tell his story, and he was given a chance to do so the next evening, at the steading where they would spend the night. His performance was effective in winning the family's heart, and each night after that it was the same in the other homes where they stayed. Bragason's stories were loved, but Forsetason's story was very personal, demonstrating his power of seeing and lifting the fears of those who listened to him. He used his drum and beat it steadily and quietly in the rhythm of his voice as he told his story, but at the point when the outlaw swung his sword, he hit the drum especially loud, and then there would be silence, and the listeners would all jump at this.

He told the story: "Early one morning, soon after sunrise, I left our farm hut to take our sheep up on the hill behind the hut, something I think all young boys have experienced, but then I heard some rustling in the nearby bushes. I thought at first it might be a boar, but three men, two with wooden clubs and one with a rusty sword, rushed out toward me. Heim, my dog, growled but kept his distance. I was unable to run because of the terrain and my sheep blocked my route of escape. All I remember is that the one with the rusty sword got to me first. According to my wound, his first swing hit me across my face. He must have left me for dead when they took the sheep. I remembered nothing until some time later when I opened my eyes—or rather, one eye—and found myself lying on my sleeping platform with a beautiful and kind woman looking down into my face. I eventually learned that her name was Vanadisdottir, and that she had a magical touch for healing. My mother was sobbing nearby, believing that I was dead or close to death. I heard my father call my name, Thord, the name he wanted for me because he had always wanted his son to be a warrior. What really amazed everyone was that thanks to the care of Vanadisdottir my wounds did not fester or fill with puss. I was told that when Heim ran home excited and barking, and my parents followed him back to where they found me, I was close to death.

"Two years after this happened Vanadisdottir visited again, at a time when we were still troubled by outlaws. This time they stole our one ram. By now, though, Vanadisdottir had taught me how to see what others could not see, and so by this seeing we found and retrieved the stolen ram. Since then I have spent much time with her and I have learned other powers of seiðr—dreaming, stalking like a cat, seeing into the future, and learning the runes. I am now journeying with Bragason to learn the magic of storytelling. I am basically a shepherd and I especially love sheep. As we came to your steading I could see that you have two sheep that are about to lamb. One is going to lamb tomorrow morning before sunrise. She has triplets, and the second to be born will be a ram. But he is breech, not facing the right way to find his way out, and without your help he and the mother will die."

This part was serious and was meant to impress the listeners, so his facial expressions were not of the greatest importance. He wanted the family to see beyond his appearance to hear what he had to tell them.

The next morning before sunrise Forsetason heard the sheep bleating and went out to her. The ewe had already given birth to a lamb and was struggling with the second. The farmer was there, but he did not know what to do to help her. So the young traveler reached his hand up into her and could feel the lamb's head, but not the forelegs. He pushed the lamb back up and let his fingers follow down and around the shoulders to the front legs and was able to easily pull the feet forward. From this position the lamb easily slid out. All were pleased with his help and gave them cheese and bread for an especially nourishing lunch.

The two travelers passed through the distant parts of Olaf's domain before reaching the domain of Hygelac, king of the Geats. On the way, Forsetason told his story many times, and in each home he was able to practice his skill of seeing and foretelling something that would be helpful to the family. Upon entering the domain of Hygelac, they soon discovered that Hygelac's father, Hreðel, had died of grief because of the death of his oldest son. Forsetason's arrival was beginning to be known throughout the countryside because he had been telling his story everywhere he went. This story carried them safely through Hygelac's domain, to the place where the many carved stones that Bragason had spoken of were to be found. It was an area that many years later would be called Tanum. There Forsetason learned to read these stone carvings and the stories they told of ancient battles. By then it was late fall, and this traveling pair planned to spend the winter with King Hygelac. And though he learned many of Bragason's stories during the winter they spent with the Geat king, Forsetason was to learn another story, the second of his own stories—a story of Beowulf, who was the nephew of Hygelac.

He first met Beowulf, the famous berserker who had raced that giant of a man Breca across the sea, in the royal settlement of King Hygelac. When Forsetason, in the days when he was known as Thord, had rescued Breca, who had washed ashore at Scania during his famous race, he learned that Beowulf had disappeared in this race and was believed to have drowned. Now Forsetason learned what had really happened: Beowulf had swum on to the land of the Finns, and when he did not find Breca there had assumed *he* was dead.

What impressed Forsetason the most upon meeting the Geat warrior was the size and sheer strength of Beowulf. When King Hreðel died, they buried him in a royal burial mound, a mound surrounded by huge boulders set in the outline of a royal ship. These boulders were larger than the stone he had carved for Wealhtheow and Hrothgar, a stone that took six men to lift, and Beowulf was able to carry these burial mound stones all by himself. The largest, placed at what would be the bow of the ship, was to be carved by Hygelac's master stonecarver, who knew the runes well, but upon learning that Forsetason was an aspiring stone carver he was asked to help. Because the Geat stonecarver was very experienced and Forsetason had only limited experience, he had much to learn from the older master and was grateful for the opportunity.

Bragason had promised to return Forsetason to Olaf the following spring, so following that winter they left Hygelac's domain for Scania. The journey back was uneventful except for both men telling some new stories they had learned from the previous year's travels. They sojourned with some of the same people they had met along the way to the land of the Geats, so on the return trip those people now seemed much more accepting of Forsetason's appearance, and he felt their love for him.

At home, Prince Hrothgar was especially eager to hear Forsetason's stories about Beowulf. Likewise, it felt good to Forsetason to get back to his sheep that he knew and loved so much.

15

KING ATHILS'S ATTACK

Just as the narrative reaches a plateau, I again ask the most general question of the Freyr Diviner, "What happens next?" The story of Forsetason's power of seeing emerges in greater detail, and as it unfolds I pose questions about the raid on the people of Scania, an event that will provide Forsetason with much respect and fame. An unexpected visit by a flotilla of ships from Denmark, carrying news of King Healfdene's injury and illness, prompts more questions, which I put to Freyr . . .

The fall harvest was almost finished, and the sheep were growing their winter coats. One night Forsetason had another dream—perhaps more accurately a nightmare. He saw a multitude of men gathering in the woods at night, inland from the settlement. He saw three ships coming into the harbor. He awakened from this dream to hear Heim growling. He got up and went outside. Everything was quiet—too quiet. No owls hooted. No other sounds came from the woods. A sliver of a moon was high in the sky, telling him that it was still several hours before dawn. He knew his dream was still a couple of hours into the future. Because of the silence of the animals, he expected the attacking warriors were still some distance away.

Forsetason hurried down the knoll to the great hall where the warriors slept. He found Hrothgar and quietly woke him to tell him of the impending attack. Though Hrothgar was not sure he should believe this shepherd boy, he did know that it was an opportunity to test the preparedness of his men. He quickly and quietly woke them, not feeding the fires because that would give their alertness away. With the warning that the attack would be both from inland and the sea, he divided the men. He told Hailgesson to hold his fifty men in the great hall and only when the ships were close enough to the land to see the activities of the settlement were his men to run down to the ramparts along the shore. That way the approaching ships would believe that their arrival was unexpected. Hrothgar himself took fifty men to defend the rear of the settlement, which was less defensible. Should the men move up into the woods? Would there be time? Should they hide behind the outbuildings and animal shelters? It was Forsetason who suggested that they hide in the sheep pen. The pen was a few meters north of the settlement and was made of posts and slats that would provide some protection to the men squatting behind it. He knew that the men in the pen would agitate the sheep, but he believed that he and Heim could keep them to one side with the hope of keeping them quiet. He suggested that Hrothgar have his men move as quietly and slowly as possible so as to not agitate the sheep and create a stir that would alert the enemy.

Hrothgar sent a dozen men up to Forsetason's hut, which was north and west of the sheep pen. The hut was unassuming and appeared in disuse. He sent another twenty men to the east to hide in or near the bastu at the top of the ravine. He believed that the invaders would be arriving from the east and would need to pass above the bastu. The men in the bastu could then attack from the rear. If the warriors attacked from the woods between the hut and the bastu, Hrothgar's men would attack them from the rear and on both sides. He ordered them to hold off on their attack until the enemy was even with or just past their hiding place. All of Hrothgar's strategy was based on what Forsetason had seen and told him, and indeed this is exactly what transpired.

As dawn broke, everyone in the settlement could see the warships in the harbor. The banner of the lead ship was that of the king of Upsala, the cruel Athils. His army of Swedes was known to be powerful, and this power was threatened by the alliance between the leaders of

Denmark and Scania. Athils expected that the ships openly approaching the harbor would distract Olaf's men, and that they would not be
expecting an attack from the rear.

As Hailgesson, Olaf's first retainer and the chief of his warriors, led
his men in a charge down from the great hall, they beat on their shields
to intimidate the approaching war fleet. It was apparent that they were
outnumbered three to one, with fifty men on each of the three ships,
but the men running ashore would be far more vulnerable. Meanwhile,
the invaders charging from the rear were from two ships that were
pulled ashore to the east, not far from Gudvi's family farm that had
been burned down. The invaders from the rear numbered about one
hundred.

The battle played out as Forsetason had seen in his vision. The
Swedish warriors from the woods were not aware of the trap they were
entering. The battle was fierce, and Hrothgar lost some men, but the
Swedish shield quickly broke as a result of attacks from both sides and
the rear. When the invaders saw that the defending army was behind
the sheep pen they continued to charge toward the pen, but they had to
raise their shields to climb the fence, which made them vulnerable from
between the slats of the fence. This force quickly crumbled, too.

Meanwhile, unbeknownst to anyone in Scania, King Healfdene had
been wounded while sparring with one of his retainers, a minor wound
on his left arm that subsequently became infected. At this point the
king was bedridden with a high fever. The Danish king—actually, it
was his queen—had decided to recall Hrothgar to Zealand in preparation for Hrothgar to be named king should the king die. The Danes
dispatched two ships to Olaf's settlement, with Prince Halga in command. Halga was to remain with Olaf, taking Hrothgar's place, and
Hrothgar and his new bride were to return to Zealand. On his way to
Scania, Halga had stopped briefly at the western harbor, and there one
of Olaf's ships out on patrol joined the entourage, sailing into Olaf's
settlement. Thus the morning of the attack, three more ships appeared
unexpectedly on the horizon and sailed into the harbor.

Athils saw what was happening and knew that he had only one option—to retreat. His three ships turned to leave, giving Hailgesson the opportunity to lead his fifty men onboard one of their own ships in pursuit of the Swedish king. Halga's ships joined in the pursuit, and the four allied ships attacked the last of the enemy fleeing the harbor. Thus Athils limped home from this misadventure with only two of his warships.

The victory was celebrated that evening with mixed feelings. All were proud of having vanquished Athils, and once again Forsetason was a hero. It seemed that no one could deny the powers of their seiðrmaðr, not even the followers of Thor. Unfortunately, six of Olaf's men had died and several others had been wounded. Vanadisdottir treated the wounded men with an herbal broth to drink and a poultice made of a mixture of herbs wrapped in a kulsukker leaf.

The reunion of the two Skjǫldung princes was also tinged with mixed feelings. They were pleased to be together again, but Hrothgar joined with his brother in their sorrow over the news of the grave illness of their father. It was necessary that Hrothgar make haste to return to his father's side. All knew that Wealhtheow was expected to go with him, and with her, Vanadisdottir. Olaf and Gunheid were sad at the departure of their beloved daughter, Wealhtheow. But with Healfdene expected to die, plans had to be made fast. Hrothgar would leave the following morning. Prince Halga had hoped that Vanadisdottir would travel with them because with her medicine she might still be able to bring Healfdene back to health. The young girl Gudvi would go with her. In this way Forsetason would be losing several close friends and allies, but Vanadisdottir believed that his skills of seiðr, now a proven fact, were such that he could take care of himself and offer Olaf protection. Furthermore, Gunheid believed in the gods and goddesses of the Vanir, and Forsetason knew he could count on her support. The priestess instructed Forsetason on how to care for the rest of the wounded retainers. While watching the young seiðrmaðr clean one man's wounds, another warrior, in a delirium, attacked the shepherd, and had to be restrained. Vanadisdottir had confidence that with Forsetason's help, all the wounded would recover. The priestess and shepherd both knew that there would be frequent journeys between the two settlements, and that they would see each other again soon.

To accommodate the additional travelers going back to Healfdene's settlement, several of the crew members of Olaf's ship were given horses to ride to the west harbor. Several of Halga's warriors were to remain with their prince in Scania as his support, so there was enough room onboard, and the next morning they all departed. The two ships made an uneventful trip back to Hleidargard, with a brief stop at the west harbor.

Upon his arrival, Hrothgar found his father in bed delirious with fever and a wound festering on his left arm. Vanadisdottir was quickly called to the king's bedside, and she went to work at what she did best. She prepared a tea for him to drink, which had to be spooned to him slowly because he was in no condition to drink it otherwise. She had several men hold him down while she opened and cleaned the festering wound and then packed it with a compress made of a kulsukker leaf and other herbs. She needed a strong man to be at his side to prevent him from tearing off the compress, and afterward she stayed with the king to speak soothing words to him.

Soon after they had arrived, the men of Healfdene's settlement started building a hall for Wealhtheow. Her hall would have two chambers. The larger, main chamber would be a congregating place for the women, with two fire pits along the center and several sleeping platforms along the sides, one for Vanadisdottir, one for Gudvi, and others for guests. A smaller side chamber would be Wealhtheow's private sleeping chamber, with a larger sleeping platform to accommodate both her and Hrothgar. During the construction Wealhtheow stayed in the hall of her sister-in-law, Signy. Hrothgar spent much of his time in the largest royal hall of his father, though once Wealhtheow's hall was completed he preferred to retreat there, to be with his bride.

Meanwhile, thanks to Vanadisdottir's ministrations, Healfdene was starting to recover. He stayed in bed in Queen Sigrid's hall, where he received the gentle care of women, though his retainers would frequently look in on him to pay their respects. The king was now sleeping more peacefully. The hope of all was that he would recover fully. In his absence, the men sworn to him spent much of their days training with Hrothgar. Most of the men had trained with him before he left to get married anyway, and so now they welcomed his return. Hrothgar became acquainted with a small group of new men who had joined Healfdene in his absence. So he now had nearly 300 men, compared to Olaf's 100, with an additional eighty posted at the west harbor.

16

HROTHGAR
BECOMES KING

The visions I receive next as I sit in the Freyr Diviner posture portend great change in the lives of Hrothgar and Wealhtheow—visions that come as a response to the questions "What will be the role of Prince Hrothgar during Healfdene's illness?" "What will happen if Healfdene should die?" and "What will this new life be like for Wealhtheow?" The answers to each of these questions lead to other, more specific questions, as the story unfolds . . .

Hrothgar sat at the bedside of his father, King Healfdene. The king was sleeping soundly; his wounded arm was no longer inflamed and hot, and his fever had broken. The people of his kingdom were hopeful that he would recover fully. He was a most benevolent and beloved king. Though everyone knew the king's heir, Hrothgar, possessed the same qualities as his father, all wished for the old king's return to his high seat in the great hall.

While Hrothgar sat at his father's side, his father opened his eyes and saw his son sitting beside the bed. He lay quietly for a long time before speaking, but when he spoke he told his son that though he felt his head was now clear and he was rested, he knew why his arm had been injured while sparring with his men: he realized he had lost his agility, his speed. He should have easily avoided being hit, but he had become too slow. Other warriors who become slow in this way were given land and left the retinue of their king to become farmers. For the sake of the kingdom and the people, Hrothgar needed to become the new king. He advised his son, "As I grow older I will be at your side, and if I feel it necessary I will give you advice. But I am old and will not live forever; it is time for you to sit in the high seat in our great hall."

Hrothgar remained silent. He did not know what to say. He was worried, but waited until later that night, when he was in his bedchamber with Wealhtheow, to tell her about his worries.

"My father, the king, is set on dying of old age. He does not think he will live much longer and does not feel capable of dying in battle as a great warrior. He is set on going to Hel's domain and will be greatly missed in Valhalla." As she listened to her husband, Wealhtheow held another belief but knew that at this time she could not convince her husband of any other possibility. She needed to take this concern to Vanadisdottir, but it would have to wait until morning. Now was the time to just be with Hrothgar in his worry.

The next morning, after Hrothgar left to return to his father's side, Wealhtheow called Vanadisdottir into her chambers. Upon telling the priestess what the king had told his son, and about Hrothgar's deep concern, Vanadisdottir went to the king's bedside and checked his wound. It was healing nicely. She then spoke to him, and Hrothgar was there to hear what she had to say.

"I have an important story to tell you. I am a priestess of Freyja, a goddess of the Vanir. The Vanir are much older than the Æsir, the warrior gods led by Odin. The Vanir are the children of Moðir, who is the sister of Bor, Odin's father. Thus Moðir is Odin's aunt. As you know, the Æsir and Vanir fought, but their battles always resulted in a stalemate. You may not know the reason why. The Æsir's warriors are the strongest, but they still could not win these battles. The Vanir are stronger in other ways, in the ways of magic. You know the story of Fenrir the wolf and what it took to restrain him? One of the fibers in the magical binding was the sinew of a bear, a fiber of great physical strength. But it took other fibers too, fibers that were strong but in other ways, ways the Vanir know, ways of magic, for the Vanir do not depend only on physical strength—in fact, none of them are exceptionally strong. They depend on such things as the sound a cat makes when it walks, a stalking strength that allows them to see what Odin and Thor are unable to see. One thing they can see is into the minds of others, something we call *intuition*. They know and respect the powers of the animals, and that all animals have their own powers, powers often greater than those of humans. Through their compassion and understanding of all flora and fauna, all of nature is on their side. It is my understanding of the flora, an understanding that I learned in my training in becoming a priestess of Freyja, that healed you. It is Forsetason's understanding of spirit journeying, journeying that he calls *dreaming* and *seeing*, that saved Breca and warned Olaf of the raiders that attacked above the west harbor and the attack of Athils.

"There is much of this magic that I don't know, and Forsetason does not know, but we continue to learn. One story that is important for you to hear is the story of Griðbustaðr, the Dwelling Place of Peace, the place where those who die with an understanding of the importance of compassion and care for others go after death. Those who have learned how to direct their spirit in journeying can travel to this place of rest and peace after death. And learning to direct your spirit is not difficult. It only takes moving your attention to the place of harmony within you, your hvilðgarðr, the place in your abdomen just below your umbilicus.

"As warriors, you know this place within you as your place of balance, that spot that you drop to plant yourself firmly so that you cannot be moved. But that is only one use of your hvilðgarðr. Right now, if you move your attention to that spot, you will feel a sense of harmony, a sense of quiet peace. It is in this way of feeling harmony that animals come to me without fear, knowing that I will not harm them. There is so much I can tell you, so much for you to learn, both of you, but you already understand much of what I am telling you because of your compassion, care, and concern for others. Gefjon knows about Griðbustaðr because she was originally one of the Vanir. I have faith that upon your death you will go to this place of peace and beauty."

With these words, Vanadisdottir placed one hand on Healfdene's hand and the other on Hrothgar's. She left her hands there for a moment before she left the hall and left them to their own thoughts.

That night, when Hrothgar went to Wealhtheow's bedchamber, he did not seem as worried, and they talked of when Healfdene might be strong enough to return to his high seat in the great hall and speak to his retainers about his plans. This soon happened a few days later, when Healfdene announced to all that it was time for Hrothgar to assume the throne, and that plans to this effect should commence.

When having to make important decisions, it was Healfdene's practice to climb to the top of the burial mound of his father, Beow, where he would sit to think. Sometimes he would have his champion or someone else with him, with whom he could discuss what needed to be done or to make plans. And so in planning for elevating Hrothgar to king, he asked his son to join him on the mound and spoke to him:

"When I became king, my father, Beow, had already died. He died in battle protecting this land of the Skjǫldung. I took his sword, and with little fanfare waved it, proclaiming that I was now king. There was never a time that this land was without a king. Things are different now. It will be important to turn my sword over to you and do so on top of this mound. Who should be here with us? Your mother, your wife, and maybe a few steps down the mound, your bother, Halga, who will be the leader of our retainers and our warriors. I expect the warriors will be standing at the base of the mound, watching from a short distance. The passing of my sword needs to be done with our right hands on our Mjollnir, in praise of Thor; we should call on Odin for his wisdom and farsightedness. Our men need to honor these gods for their strength in defending us."

While this was going on, Wealhtheow and Vanadisdottir were also talking. They understood what Odin and Thor meant to these men and recognized their need to honor these gods of the Æsir. Vanadisdottir knew that this time she needed to stand back, on the sidelines, because her thinking and beliefs were so much different from theirs. She knew that the king would call on her when he needed her magic, but now was not such a time. Though his men depended on the strength of Thor, the king also depended on the wisdom of Odin, and the wisdom of compassion for his people, compassion that he attributed to Gefjon. Vanadisdottir hoped that Hrothgar, as king, would call on this goddess too—something that Wealhtheow had suggested to him, since without her this land would not exist.

Time was needed for word to be sent for the return of Halga for the ceremony. Olaf and Gunheid would also attend. Thus the date was set for ten days hence. During Olaf's absence Hailgesson would be a very capable leader of Olaf's men, and with the visions of Forsetason to aid him, the safety of Scania during this time would be assured.

In this way, ten days later Hrothgar became king, and during the crowning they all paid tribute to three deities, Odin, Thor, and Gefjon. Afterward, Vanadisdottir suggested to Wealhtheow that two memorial stones were needed—one dedicated to the greatness of the Skjǫldung king Healfdene, and one to King Hrothgar in honor of this day. When Queen Sigrid passed this suggestion along to Healfdene, he was in favor of the idea and asked who should carve the stones. The only stonecarver known to the king was Forsetason.

Thus it was that when Olaf returned to Scania, he sent Forsetason on one of his ships back to Hleidargard. And as a result of what he had learned from the stonecarver of King Hygelac in the land of the Geats, the stones Forsetason carved for Healfdene and Hrothgar were especially beautiful, and each took six men to carry. The stones were placed at the entrance to the king's great hall.

17

HEALFDENE'S LAST DAYS AND THE SIGHTING OF GRENDEL

As Hrothgar becomes king with many new responsibilities, the lives of his father, Healfdene, and his wife, Wealhtheow undergo great changes. Questions are asked of the spirit of Freyr about how their lives change. The appearance of Grendel, a curious-looking monster, opens the door to many more questions, the answers to which prove illuminating. The death of Healfdene causes some concern for his followers since he did not die a hero in battle, yet Vanadisdottir finds a way to alleviate their concerns with her stories of the Vanir, as revealed to me while standing in the powerful Hallstatt Warrior pose. This Realm of the Dead posture brings me closer to Healfdene in his death . . .

As the new king, one of Hrothgar's first tasks was to finish the planned new settlement at the east harbor, across from and above the west harbor of King Olaf. With this new settlement across the strait, the men at both settlements could now begin to patrol and collect a toll from ships passing in the strait. A required payment of a nominal sum was expected from merchants who passed, and raiders could be stopped and confronted. It did not take long for word to spread that raiders were not welcome. Hrothgar and Olaf were quite pleased with this arrangement, which increased their wealth and protected their people.

The everyday illnesses and injuries of the people in the royal settlement of Hleidargard kept Vanadisdottir busy, and young Gudvi was learning much by being at her side to assist the priestess. The new queen, as she always had done from an early age, still spent time with her guvernante, visiting and getting to know the families of Hleidargard. Her compassionate and outgoing nature brought Wealhtheow close to everyone in the community, and they were growing to love and respect her. Wealhtheow's new sister and trusted friend, Signy, was of great help to her in introducing her to these families, letting her know of their special needs and explaining their interrelationships. Though Hrothgar was away much of the time, at night when he was at home Wealhtheow would listen to his concerns, and on some evenings she would go to the great hall to sit at his side. When she did, Hrothgar's retainers would act more courtly; otherwise, with their tendency to drink large quantities of mead, their usual behavior was more raucous.

Healfdene spent much of his time strolling the royal settlement, watching the men practice their battle skills, sitting in the great hall next to and behind the high seat of his son, the king, and wandering down the hill from the great hall, past the bog, and up the other side, to the top of the burial mound of his father, Beow. Vanadisdottir would observe him, and when she saw him walking down toward the bog where often deer and other animals were found because it was a place for them to drink, she would join him. He always seemed pleased when she sat with him. She would sit watching the animals, and as she would move her attention to her center of harmony the animals would come closer. The king began to notice how the deer especially would come closer. When he commented on this, she told him to move his attention to his center of harmony, and when he did, the deer came very close to both of them. Vanadisdottir picked a handful of grass and held it out to the deer, and after a while they ventured close enough to take the grass from her hand. Soon, feeding the deer in this way became a great love of Healfdene, and he discovered he could do it even when Vanadisdottir was not with him. In this way he felt great harmony with the earth, or as Vanadisdottir would say, with the Great Mother. He would pick a handful of grain from the grasses around the pond and soon he had the ravens coming to eat out of his hand, too. When the ravens came to him he praised Odin and the god's two ravens.

He would then go to the top of his father's mound to visit with his father and talk to the gods about the meaning and pleasures of life, appreciating this sense of harmony as he grew old. Wealhtheow heard about this from Vanadisdottir and told her husband about how his father was feeding the deer and the ravens. Hrothgar did not know what to think of this, but one day he saw his father sitting by the bog and joined him. At first, the deer and the ravens kept their distance, looking at Hrothgar with curiosity. But when his father told him to relax and move his attention to his center of harmony, it did not take long for the birds and deer to approach them both. Though this fascinated Hrothgar, he felt he did not have time for such "play" when there were so many important things to do in protecting and providing for the people of his realm. Yet in honor of his father's newfound love for the deer he named his new and expanded great hall Heorot, which means "hart," the male of the red deer.

Though Vanadisdottir told no one, late in the fall when she sat with Healfdene by the bog calling the animals, she felt the presence of something else, and letting her eyes see as others cannot, she observed a large, hairy, humanlike creature hiding behind the trees on the other side of the pond. The appearance of this creature caused chills to run down her spine; nevertheless she watched with curiosity, in the same way that the creature was watching her with curiosity. Over the next few days she saw it coming closer, but it never openly revealed itself.

Then the day came late in the fall when the cold weather prevented Healfdene from sitting by the water's edge. He went to the great hall, but he did not appreciate the noise of the men so he returned to his own hall, where he lay down on his sleeping platform, fell asleep, and did not again wake up. Missing his father, Hrothgar went out in search of him and found him in his quarters having passed away. Though his death was not unexpected, it nevertheless brought grief to the kingdom.

Though a ship burial was generally expected for royalty, a couple of months earlier Healfdene had expressed his preference for cremation on a funeral pyre. In this way he felt that his spirit would rise up and find its way to the place of peace rather than to the domain of Hel, where the burial ship would certainly take him. Again, this decision perplexed Hrothgar, who wanted to stay with tradition. Sometimes when a king died he would be placed on a ship that would be pushed out to sea to take him to the next world; other times a ship was pulled onto land and the king's body placed on the ship, which was then buried in a large mound of earth. When a ship was not available, the king or chieftain would be buried and large burial stones would be placed around the grave in the outline of a sea vessel. Though Hrothgar had heard that in ancient times kings were placed on funeral pyres, that was a long time ago. But because these were the last wishes of his father, a pyre was build. To do this, a ship was pulled in from the water onto the land, its bow turned to face north. A first layer of logs, about ten inches in diameter, was laid in the bottom of the ship in the east, the spring of life, in remembrance of the birth of the former king. The next layer of logs was laid in a southerly direction, in remembrance of Healfdene's childhood and development, the summer of life. The third layer was placed from the west, to remember his years as king, the fall and sunset of life. The fourth layer was placed from the north, to remember his elder years of winter, a time of preparation for rebirth in the spring, a rebirth in the place that a person goes following death. The last and fifth layer of logs was for carrying him to the upper world. When a torch was set to this stack of logs, they would form a very hot bed of glowing embers, hot enough for cremating a body.

Healfdene's body was placed on top of the logs, and a fire was set under and around the ship. His closest retainers tended the fire, continually adding wood until the flesh of the king's body was gone and the bones were glowing as red as the embers beneath it. The fire burned for two days. His final ashes could be seen rising into the sky and eventually settling again on the earth, and in this way returning to Mother Earth. Watching the ashes had not been done for many generations, but as Hrothgar watched them he felt a strange appreciation for the old ways.

Because no burial mound or stone was there to remember this third, great king of Denmark, Hrothgar again called on Forsetason to carve a stone in remembrance of his father.

As the days passed and winter set in, when Vanadisdottir had no other pressing duties, she could be seen sitting by the bog where she had once sat with Healfdene. She was very curious about the hairy creature she had seen across the pond, and she still would get an occasional glimpse of him. The first time she saw him after the king's death, he was standing by a tree pounding his chest as if in grief, grief for this great and compassionate king. She felt there must have been some sort of bond between this monster and the king, though this she did not understand. To this monster she gave the name Grendel, a name that she had heard spoken by the outlying farmers of the kingdom. Grendel no longer seemed to be hiding himself from her, yet he stayed on the other side of this shallow body of water. She did not share her experience even with Wealhtheow. She knew that if Hrothgar or his men knew of Grendel, a party of his men would track the creature down, intent no doubt on killing it. It would be seen as a threat to the community, though Vanadisdottir did not feel any sort of threat.

18

THE EARLY YEARS
OF HROTHGAR'S REIGN

There is seemingly no end to the questions that can be asked of the Freyr Diviner—questions about King Hrothgar and the tremendous responsibility he now holds in maintaining alliances with other chieftains, keeping his retainers in peak condition, and providing for and protecting his people. Queen Wealhtheow also has new responsibilities: a new baby to care for and her duty as queen to reach out to the people of the domain and to be a gracious hostess to visiting chieftains. Vanadisdottir's responsibilities also expand greatly beyond her earlier responsibility as guvernante to Wealhtheow—she is now regarded as a priestess and healer for the whole realm. Again, the story flows on, with many answers given to my questions about life in ancient Denmark . . .

After finishing construction of the settlement at the east harbor, Hrothgar set about maintaining the harbor and collecting tolls from those who passed through the strait, stopping raiders, and otherwise protecting those who lived along the eastern border of his kingdom. He understood what needed to be done because he had maintained other outposts and collected tolls and protected the people who lived along the other two major straits of Denmark, between Juteland and Fyn, and between Fyn and Gefjon's island of Zealand.

Hrothgar's father had formed alliances with many of the kings and chieftains of Denmark. All the chieftains of Gefjon's island had pledged alliances with Healfdene, as had most of the chieftains of Fyn, the island between Gefjon's island and the land of the Jutes. A few of the Jute kings also saw the advantage of aligning themselves with Healfdene. At first, some kings resisted joining the alliance, and Healfdene had to call on the strength of his army of warriors to convince them that it was to their advantage to join him. In some cases battles had been necessary to bring about peace, but the strength of Healfdene's army had been sufficient to bring any resistant kings into the alliance. At first, some of them thought that paying tribute to Healfdene was unfair, but they soon realized that the strength of Healfdene's warriors, in addition to their own, provided ample protection from raiders and other enemies. Raiders were hearing stories of the strength of this unified army and stayed away from the Danish islands. Healfdene's army was considered the strongest army at the time.

Another strength of the kingdom that Hrothgar inherited was that Healfdene had been very open-handed in distributing his wealth by giving treasures to visiting chieftains and armbands to warriors who showed exceptional valor. Most of those who had at one time had considered themselves kings, like Olaf, were now regarded as chieftains under King Healfdene, though by their own people they were still sometimes called king. They realized that the tribute they paid was often returned to them as gifts and rewards, so they, too, would take gifts when visiting the king. Except for the most greedy of the chieftains, most of them appreciated the benevolence of Healfdene. As a result of this system based on tribute and reward, with few exceptions Healfdene's kingdom now extended from the land of the Friesnians to the south of the land of the Jutes. And now, with the alliance with Olaf, it expanded across southern Sweden, to the land of the Ynglings.

It was now Hrothgar's responsibility to win over those few remaining chieftains who had resisted the alliance that his father had formed. It was Hrothgar's brother Halga's responsibility to maintain the army; Sœvil, Signy's husband and Hrothgar's brother-in-law, would collect the tribute from those chieftains. In his travels to collect tribute, Sœvil took a small band of warriors with him for protection, but he did not want to appear threatening by traveling with a larger army of men. It was his job to represent Hrothgar correctly by upholding the friendships between these leaders. The king also made regular visits to his chieftains to keep alliances strong and to convey gifts of friendship to them. As a result of these alliances, the areas of outlawry between the domains of each chieftain had shrunk, such that it had become much safer to travel.

Thus, during the first few years of Hrothgar's reign the young king visited all the chieftains of his land, gaining their trust and assurance in protecting the land and convincing the remaining resistant chieftains—either through peaceful means or through a show of military force if necessary—to join the alliance. Because of this, he was gone from Hleidargard much of the time. During these times when he was away, Halga would assign other warriors to be in charge of protecting Hleidargard.

Though the king's warriors were important to him, the farming freemen who lived outside of Hleidargard were also very important, as the king depended on them for the great quantities of food consumed in the settlement. Though they rarely received armbands and other such tokens of appreciation from the king, his blacksmith made them the tools they needed for farming. The king kept a herd of sheep, because the fresh meat and wool of these animals was so greatly valued; in addition, the warriors would often go hunting and bring back deer and wild pigs. What could not be eaten in one feast was smoked and dried for later. The women enjoyed going for walks to collect nuts, berries, and herbs, but much of the other food staples, the turnips and other root crops and the grains for making bread, were grown by the farm families in the kingdom. The farmers always set aside a share of these staples for the king and his warriors in payment for the protection they provided.

Though there were certain respected women in the community whom people went to for healing, the priestess of Freyja, Vanadisdottir, was beginning to be recognized throughout the kingdom as the most skilled of the healers, and so these other healing women started going to her for advice and to learn of new herbs and ways of healing that they did not already know. Besides ministering to the warriors and their families, Vanadisdottir was often called on to visit a farm family to help them in whatever their need was.

As life went on, a farmer might have a dream that one of his sons would become a warrior for the king, but the family always had the need to keep at least one of the sons at home to help with the farm. The wish of the farmer was often to have a daughter marry a warrior, thinking that her life would be greatly improved, though that was not always the case. Farm wives were also needed, so the daughters of farmers often ended up marrying the son of another farmer. Though the life of a farmer was hard work, this work was not as dangerous as fighting with swords and spears; yet if a king was in a dire situation he might have to call on the farmers to bring their weapons to help in the fight. However, under King Hrothgar, because his army was so strong, this need to call on the farmers was rare, and so the farmers were left to do their farming in peace.

Wealhtheow spent most of her time getting to know the other women of the settlement. Though Gudvi was now always at Vanadisdottir's side in helping her administer to the people in the settlement, Wealhtheow spent a lot of her time with her guvernante too; otherwise she was in the hall of the women, spinning, weaving, sewing, and cooking, with Signy, her sister through marriage, at her side. In all her activities, Wealhtheow listened to the stories of other women. One mother who had one son who was eleven years old was worried because her warrior husband was determined to make the boy into a warrior. The boy was smaller than other boys his age and showed no interest in fighting. His one friend was another boy born with a withered arm who everyone knew would not be a warrior, so he had become a tender of the family's sheep. Healfdall, this young boy who didn't want to fight, liked to spend his time with his friend, sitting on the hillside with the sheep. The mother did not know what to do. Wealhtheow told this mother the story of the shepherd boy Forsetason, and how important he has become to her father, High Chief Olaf, but the mother knew her son was not in the same kind of situation that caused Forsetason to become a shepherd—namely, he had not been wounded and disfigured. So what was she to do?

Wealhtheow told this mother's story to Vanadisdottir, who had already noticed the two boys sitting on the hill together watching the sheep. The next day she went down to the pond to feed one of the deer some grain she had picked, and then carried some of it with her as she walked up the hill to where the two boys were sitting. The deer followed her. She sat some distance from the boys and fed the deer while the boys watched. While she sat there one of the sheep wandered over to her, and so she gave the sheep some grain. The boys had never seen animals come to somebody as they did to Vanadisdottir and they were curious about how she did it. In this way she gained two more students for learning the ways of seiðr. She first taught them about using their center of harmony for bringing animals to them, and then how to find sheep that wander off by seeing in a different way, again using their center of harmony. She also taught them how to make and use a drum. Over the next few months they proved to be receptive students in learning these powers of magic, though Healfdall's father did not know what to think and complained about the time his son spent with her.

Then one day this father was out hunting with a friend and was gored by a wild boar and knocked into a ravine. He hit his head on a rock and was unconscious. The other hunter, his friend, could not find him and returned home without him. When Healfdall heard that his father had gone missing, he grabbed his drum and using his new powers of seeing and dreaming, took off running in the direction where the hunter had last seen his father. He sat there for a few moments beating his drum, then ran quickly to the ravine, where he found his father. His father was still unconscious but came to with a splash of water. Following not far behind was the other hunter and the boy's mother. All were impressed by how quickly Healfdall was able to find his father, an act that probably saved his father's life since he was not easily seen from the top of the ravine. After that the father became more appreciative of his son's gifts, though he would still talk about how he wished his son would become a warrior.

Because of her husband's extensive traveling, it would be eight years into her marriage to Hrothgar before Wealhtheow first became pregnant. By then Hrothgar was spending more time at home, where he met with the various chieftains and men of valor, to whom he distributed his wealth. Wealhtheow graciously played her role as queen in the ceremony of greeting the visitors and passing a cup of mead to these guests. Prince Hrethric, their first son, was born in the fall, a healthy and strong baby.

19

GRENDEL DISTURBS THE PEACE

Footprints and other sightings of the monster Grendel are becoming more numerous. Questions about what is going to happen next are not necessary since the story of Grendel's attack of Heorot, the great hall of King Hrothgar, is well documented in the ancient poem *Beowulf*. But we now know that Vanadisdottir has developed an understanding relationship with this creature from the past, and so my questions concern what she is going to do as a result of Grendel's attack. These questions are posed while sitting in ecstatic trance with the Freyr Diviner, and the answers I receive provide a new dimension to the ancient epic poem *Beowulf* . . .

Three years after the birth of Prince Hrethric, eleven years into Hrothgar's reign, the king became a father again, this time to another healthy, strong boy, named Hrothmund. The days were becoming shorter and winter solstice was only a few weeks away. Wealhtheow was awakened by Gudvi, who brought Hrothmund to her. The three-month-old baby was hungry and seeking her breast. He was always hungry. Though most women of high rank, especially queens, would not nurse their babies but instead have a wet nurse for them, Wealhtheow wanted to nurse her sons herself and was encouraged to do so by Vanadisdottir. Both mother and priestess wanted the children to become bonded to their mother in this way, with the hope that they might feel closer to these women and therefore want to learn more of the old ways. Normally a young prince might be fostered out to another family who would raise him to adulthood, something that Wealhtheow would never consider. Hrothgar had already left Wealhtheow's bed to go to the great hall to greet his men as they awakend, and Vanadisdottir was out tending to another expectant mother. Once Gudvi put the baby prince in his mother's arms, the girl asked permission to leave so that she could run to be at Vanadisdottir's side for the birth.

In the great hall there was something of a commotion. One of the men had left the hall in the middle of the moonlit night to relieve himself and had seen at the edge of the woods a figure that appeared to be somewhat human, with arms that hung halfway down its legs. The creature was very hairy and was jumping up and down. The retainer took a few steps in its direction when the creature turned and disappeared into the woods. The man went back into the hall but there was no one awake for him to tell what he had seen—everyone was snoring in a drunken stupor. He had to wait until morning when the men began to wake up. Then he and several of the men went outside to examine the place where this creature had been seen. The dry earth had been disturbed but no footprints were clearly seen. Then, as they walked a short distance into the woods, they clearly saw a large footprint in the damp earth, in a space between fallen leaves. No one knew what to think. When the king came into the hall, he was told the story and taken out to see the footprint. They were then able to follow a trail of sorts that became clear once the men knew what to look for—broken twigs on the trees and brush and disturbed leaves on the ground. The trail led north, towards the fjord, and then down into a ravine that separated the great hall from the burial mound of King Beow. There, because of the sand, rocks, and a new light snowfall that covered everything, the trail was lost.

Word of sighting of this creature spread quickly, and soon the news reached Vanadisdottir. She knew the men were talking about Grendel. Later in the day she had a break from her duties and went down to the bog and sat, hoping to see Grendel. He did appear, again on the other side of the pond. As they saw each other Vanadisdottir began to walk toward him and he motioned for her to come closer. He stayed hidden behind the trees on the south side of the shallow pond. She saw that his arms were especially long; he had a low forehead and protruding brows above his eyes. He was naked except for long hair all over his body. When she approached him, he bent down to pick up what was the winter remains of a leaf, held it in his hand, stroked it in a very gentle way, and then pointed to Vanadisdottir. He did this several times, thus communicating to her that she was very gentle and that he liked her. He then pointed up toward the great hall and the fighting practice field next to it, swung his long arms in the air, grunting and jumping up and down. She understood—he was telling her that he thought the men of the hall were crazy. She nodded yes to him and smiled. He understood her response. He then turned and quickly disappeared into the brush beyond the pond. When she looked into the brush she could see the entrance to a cave. This knowledge she kept secret, knowing that Grendel trusted her.

Back in the hall, the men were still talking about Grendel and didn't know what to think. Some thought that their comrade was just imagining things and that it must have been another animal, maybe a boar, though the large footprint they had seen was certainly not a boar's. Most of the men had gone onto the practice field to stay prepared for any battle, and some thought about the possibility of having to fight this creature.

The rest of that short day was uneventful, and the men returned to the hall for another evening of revelry. The new king had expanded the size of the great hall, Heorot, and the new space made the hall especially suited for festivities for the men, who now numbered about three hundred. The women carried in the food, laid it out on a long table, and the eating and drinking commenced. After an evening of eating, drinking, and comradery, and after the king retired to the hall of his queen, a few of the men who had wives also left the hall to go to the huts that they had built for themselves and their families. The women who had served the food left to return to the hall of the women, though several remained to continue pouring mead for the men. These young women, their hormones flowing, enjoyed such raucous evenings. They were looking for husbands, and as the night wore on they often found a spot in the darker corners of the great hall to lie with a man, not always the man of their future. That is why a large number of the children of Hleidargard did not know their fathers. Though the girls and the infant boys stayed in the hall of the women, as the boys grew older, to the age of four or five, they were no longer welcome in the hall and then lived in a hall built for boys. By age twelve, when they got their first swords, they were sometimes allowed to sleep with the other men in the great hall.

As the night wore on, the intoxicated men in the great hall stumbled around and found places on the floor, where they fell asleep, while those who were less drunk unrolled bedrolls to make their sleep more comfortable. The hall quieted down except for the sounds of snoring and other body noises. The young women left to return to the hall of the women, laughing and telling stories of what had happened during the evening and sharing with the others the names of the men they had ended up with. As they entered the hall of the women with torn blouses and skirts, they were met with disgusted frowns by the older woman who had been through it all and no longer had a fondness for the debaucheries of the warriors. The younger women did not yet understand why they felt this way and instead thought the older women were prudes.

But on this particular night something else happened that disturbed the routine of Hleidargard. Well into the early morning hours, someone or something entered the hall, breaking the door from its hinges. It quickly began rampaging through the hall, grabbing and savagely tearing at all the men it encountered as it went through the hall. With its sharp claws it grabbed one of the men, tore open his throat, and holding him above his head, drank the blood that flowed down. At the same time with its other arm it grabbed the next man in preparation to drink his blood. After drinking his fill, he sliced open the leg of one retainer and pulled out the strong, tough leg muscle, which he then stuffed into his mouth to chew on, and then left carrying with him the legs of two other men, two in each giant hand. As the rest of the men awakend to this carnage they could see in the glow of the last embers of the central fire the shadowy and murderous monster, and those who could grabbed their swords and axes. The ones who succeeded in reaching their weapons swung them at Grendel, but none penetrated the creature's thick hide, rendering the weapons useless even for future battle. The lucky ones either snuck out or hid somewhere in the recesses of this largest of halls.

As suddenly as the creature had come, it departed. The men were left in a state of shock, with nothing to say, after they had all experienced this deadly, murderous rampage. When daylight began to shine through the smoke holes of the hall, enough to assess the damage, thirty of the men—about one out of ten—were dead, some found along the trail of blood and body parts outside the hall. When the king came into the hall he had sufficient wits about him to organize a party of men to follow the trail, which was now much easier to track because of the blood and Grendel's continued rampage through the woods, tearing up bushes and breaking branches. Again the trail led down the ravine that ran to the north of the settlement, between Heorot and the burial mound, connecting a string of ponds, the top and southernmost pond being the one at which the old king, Healfdene, and Vannisdottir had once sat to feed the deer and ravens. They followed Grendel's trail until it entered the ravine much below this pond. This time they were able to follow the trail farther down the gradual sloping ravine, to a deep pool of black water at a place before it reached the harbor on the fjord. It was on a hill overlooking this pond that King Hrothgar assigned men to stand as night sentries. They were prepared to light a signal fire at the appearance of Grendel, a fire that could be seen by the Heorot sentry.

A couple of nights later, Grendel again entered the hall and in a rampage killed several more men. Again the bloody trail was followed, and the sentry above the pond was found hanging from a dead tree, impaled on a branch that protruded from his chest.

The next day a ship arrived from Scania with the report that Forsetason had seen what had happened several nights before in a dream. From what he saw in his dream it was clear that Grendel's wrath was the result of the nightly festivities that took place in the great hall, and was not directed at the quiet and peaceful activities of the farmstead families that lived in the smaller huts, or at the hall of women and the young boys' hall at Hleidargard.

And as word of the monster's activities spread throughout the north, many champions of Hrothgar, as well as champions of other chieftains, took up the challenge to rid the king of Grendel. None were successful. It seemed the monster's body, limbs, and claws were made of iron, and his strength could overpower any challenger, or even a number of champions who together would try to take on the creature.

All of this caused King Hrothgar considerable grief. He was the greatest and most powerful king of Denmark, yet even he had to hide at night in the hall of his wife, Queen Wealhtheow. She understood his frustration at his powerlessness against the monster, but she also had some understanding as to what caused the fury of Grendel: he was a creature from a previous era who valued the gentle and loving world of the Great Mother and disdained the warring aggression of the world in which he now had to live. He was the last of his kind, with no others who understood or supported him. But with hundreds of warriors believing in the supremacy of physical strength, the queen's beliefs, if she had spoken them, would have fallen on deaf ears. The king in his compassion, and hearing the story of Forsetason, had some understanding of this monster too, yet to keep his respect as a leader in the warrior world in which they now lived, he needed to keep his men in peak physical condition without having doubts regarding their strength and fighting skills.

20

THE SILVER LINING

While writing about Queen Wealhtheow in an altered state of consciousness, using the ecstatic trance postures to give direction to my experiences, the posture I have used most frequently has been the Freyr Diviner. However, something different happens on Sunday morning, August 11, 2013. Though I first ask Freyr about what I need to know about the queen and Vanadisdottir for this chapter, he quickly tells me that today I need to use the Freyja Initiation posture (see page 96). I change postures, and Freyja leads me in an important and unexpected direction. In my previous book, *Baldr's Magic,* I identified the Freyja posture as an initiation posture of death and rebirth; but today I feel a very different energy in this posture, an energy that is categorized by Felicitas Goodman and Belinda Gore as female healing energy. This is the energy of Freyja that is used by Vanadisdottir. Yet the experience I have personally is that of death and rebirth—the death of my feelings of hopelessness for the aggressive nature of men, and the birth of hope that women, even in these very patriarchal times, can still exert a nurturing influence.

We know from the story of Beowulf that the people of King Hrothgar's domain lived for twelve years under the threat of Grendel. This threat greatly changed how people lived, and the nature of these changes are revealed through the questions I ask while sitting in the posture of Freyr or standing in the posture of Freyja, the brother and sister god and goddess of the far north . . .

Grendel's relentless war on Hrothgar's warriors greatly demoralized Denmark's greatest and most powerful king. As a result of the ongoing torment, the king and his men were forced to change their ways. After gathering in the great hall for their evening meal—and considerably less drinking and merriment than before the arrival of Grendel—the men retreated to the outlying huts they had built for themselves and their families, where they spent the night safe from any attack by the vengeful monster. This new practice would go on for twelve years. Over the course of those twelve years more and more men found wives with whom to share their thatched hut, and those who remained single spent time alone in huts they had built for themselves or in the hidden corners of the great hall, where they questioned their lives.

What was the role of Vanadisdottir, the priestess of Freyja, in this disenchanted community? She knew that she was unable to influence or even tell the men about the fact that she knew that Grendel was never a threat to those who could show him some compassion and understanding—after all, this was not their nature in facing an enemy. But she could talk to the women of the community and influence them in bringing their families together when their husbands, the fathers of their children, returned home to their huts each evening. She could assist the women in playing a nurturing role to help heal the families and strengthen the bonds within the family. Until now, the men spent all their time in experiences that bonded them only with other men, and they viewed women mostly as sex objects. Now the men could find a greater balance in their lives—a balance that would help make King Hrothgar an even greater king, known far and wide for showing even greater compassion for and nurturance of his people.

During those twelve years, on the king's visits to the farmsteads throughout his kingdom, it became apparent to him that Grendel had no interest in harming these families, who cared for and helped one another. And though his men continued to practice their skills in combat to maintain their strength, it was no longer their entire life. King

Hrothgar no longer had the need or interest in expanding his territory by conquering other kings, but rather he found ways to create further alliances with them.

During this more restrained period, Vanadisdottir, in making her rounds of the families of Hleidargard, now felt a new freedom to tell the stories of the Vanir to the wives and children of Hrothgar's retainers, and on occasion the warriors heard the stories too, usually from their wives. She taught the wives and daughters the powers of the healing flora that were found in the area. At these times, Gudvi and Wealhtheow were at her side. Vanadisdottir had made a drum for Gudvi, who would help her by reciting "Plants of the Mother" while beating her drum, to cleanse the minds of all those present. In making Gudvi's drum, Vanadisdottir had soaked the skin in the water near where she and King Healfdene used to sit watching the animals. This water had become sacred to her. The wives saw that Queen Wealhtheow also knew and was able to tell the stories of the healing plants, and so their appreciation for their queen and her guvernante, the high priestess, grew even greater. Thus there was a silver lining to the cloud of despair that hung over Hleidargard.

On one occasion when Wealhtheow entered the hall of the woman, where they were spinning, weaving, sewing, and preparing food, she came upon a group of women talking about their husbands and how when they came home at night they would have many complaints, either about other men or often about their own inadequacies, because they were always challenging themselves to do better. The women, seeing much more of their husbands these days and hearing these complaints, did not know how to respond. So Wealhtheow told them a story about Nanna, the wife of Baldr:

"Though Baldr, the son of Odin, was compassionate and nurturing, he too had his moments of frustration. Oftentimes his conversations with Nanna were from a distance, between Asgard and Vanaheim, but they had each perfected the skill of ecstatic trance and could feel very close even at this great distance, relating to each other as if they were physically together. To her he would complain about the craziness of the warrior gods, especially about the impulsiveness of his brother Thor. But Nanna had faith in Baldr; she knew that he knew what needed to be said to his brother in these situations, and knew that she needed to say nothing—all she had to do was listen, and in their distant way of being together, hold him."

Wealhtheow told the women of Hleidargard that their husbands already knew what needed to be done to improve their own warrior skills or how to relate to the other men with whom they spent so much time. What their husbands did need, however, was for their wives to simply listen to them and love them, for it was only with their women that the men could let down their defensiveness, the kind of walls that separate people. She told them that her own husband, the king, also had a need to talk to her in this way, and he needed her to just listen and hold him. In talking out his concerns for his men and the kingdom, he usually found the needed answers within himself just by talking, provided she would just listen to him.

Most valuable to Wealhtheow, she told the women, was her ability to move her attention to her center of harmony, her hvildgarðr. She found that she would do this many times throughout the day, whenever she felt some concern or would have a question about something. And so it was this simple technique that she taught the women whenever she had a chance to do so. She especially enjoyed teaching it to the children, watching their excitement when they would find that birds and other animals would come to them and eat out of their hand when they rested in their center of harmony. If only the men could learn to appreciate this skill, as King Healfdene did in his last days. It seemed that most men did not have the patience for this. But some of the young boys of Hleidargard were excitedly learning about the power of moving their attention to their center of harmony, and Wealhtheow could not believe that they would ever forget this, even after they were old enough to get swords and had to learn to be like every other older boy and man, with their sole focus on learning the skills of combat and becoming strong.

Wealhtheow never tired of hearing and telling the story of Freyja going before Odin for the first time. When Freyja moved her attention to her center of harmony, Freki and Geri, the two wolves that sat at Odin's feet, and Hugin and Munin, the two ravens that sat on the god's shoulders, all did the unthinkable: they left their master and went to her. But to grown men such play seemed frivolous.

Vanadisdottir also talked about the value of the center of harmony, and told the women about how she held a plant over her hvilðgarðr to learn about its special use. This is something that Gudvi had been doing, and more often than not she correctly ascertained the plant's use.

It was during this period of time that Wealhtheow gave birth to the king's youngest, a daughter whom they named Freawaru. The epic poem *Beowulf* tells us that Princess Freawaru would marry the legendary warrior Ingeld.

21

VIOLENCE
AGAINST WOMEN

A week or so later I return to my favorite general question, asking Freyr to tell me what happens next while in his posture. I discover that the silver lining revealed during the previous week is only a slight sliver, as I learn much more about the lives of women in this Danish community after the coming of Grendel. I then pose my questions about how the women cope to Freyja, who as a nurturing woman has a much greater insight into the lives of women . . .

Unfortunately, the abuse of women by the men of Hleidargard was quite common. In general, husbands believed that their wives were their property and they could do with them whatever they pleased. They would come into their family hut late at night when the children and woman were sleeping and make their demands. If the woman resisted, the man would grab her, pin her to the bed, and rape her, though this was not considered a crime but rather a right of men. When an unmarried man courted a woman he wanted to be his wife, he was more likely to show a more loving and respectful attitude than he would once the woman became his wife. Some women remembered the often crude behavior on the part of the married warriors, and this made the older married women frown in disgust when the younger, unmarried women entered the women's hall early in the morning, laughing and joking about what had happened the night before.

As the men discovered that sleeping in the great hall was a threat to their lives, more and more of them started sleeping in the outlying huts, and so the instances of the abuse of women became even more frequent, and this became a great concern of Wealhtheow and Vanadisdottir. When they visited the hall of the women as they did each morning they would often find women with blackened eyes and deep bruises on their arms and their bodies. The women at first did not want to talk about what had happened, but with the increasing instances of violence against women, not knowing exactly what they could do about it, some of them finally started to speak up.

Some women would attempt to stay in the hall of the women at night, but when their husbands did not find them in their own hut they would come into the hall to find them. The hall of the women would be dark and crowded when they entered. Though the women would remain silent in their attempt to protect the man's wife, he would grab one of the women and threaten her, such that the man's wife was quick to come forward in order to protect the other woman. Upon returning to her family hut she would most certainly be beaten. On one occasion, after the husband fell asleep, his wife left and returned to the women's hall with a broken arm. Another woman set it and bound the arm to a splint before Vanadisdottir saw her the next morning. Wearing a splint and having to tell others what had happened was very humiliating for this woman, and she was unable to perform her expected duties of spinning, weaving, sewing, and preparing food for several weeks. Even her husband was embarrassed in front of the other men for what he had done, yet at the same time the other men believed he had the right to force her to give herself to him sexually.

For a woman in such a violent situation, Vanadisdottir had one suggestion: spirit travel. The woman could go within herself and temporarily leave her body and travel to some place of comfort and peace as she was being physically abused and raped. She taught the women how to first listen within their heads to the rapid beat of a drum, the sound of which would cover the noises made by the husband and carry them to their special place of peace and comfort. Learning to do this was helpful for some women when the abuse was not too extreme, but often the thought of children being in the same room and them hearing what was going on, with their need to protect them, prevented the mother from leaving her body.

One woman, though, said she found spirit journeying quite useful. On her spirit journeys she would go back to her old family farmstead, where she was in the family hut helping her mother. She could feel the embrace of her father when she ran to him when he came in from working outside. There she found a real place of peace, so different from where she lived now, though her parents were no longer alive and she did not know who now lived on her family's farmstead. After her father died they had no place to go except to Hleidargard. Her father thought that her brother would do well to become a warrior, so he practiced and eventually became one of Hrothgar's retainers. Then all he cared about was practicing combat and drinking. Her mother had died, and she now had no one left from her family.

Another wife and mother did not have such a pleasant childhood, but she found peace by journeying in spirit down to the fjord to watch the waves washing onto the shore. To her, the waves were very soothing.

Occasionally, when women would come to the woman's hall with severe injuries like broken bones, the queen would report this to Hrothgar. Her husband was a gentle and compassionate husband and father, concerned for the women of Hleidargard. He knew his men and knew they needed to be single-minded in the pursuit of strength and skills in combat, because he knew it took such a focus to be effective in battle in protecting the realm. He praised his men for their strength and was quick to give them armbands and other rewards for their valor in battle. He also knew that criticism, threats, and other such punishments were ineffective because they would hamper morale. Though he too enjoyed drinking mead with his men at the close of the day, he drank in moderation and would leave the hall before the real drinking would commence, and he knew that this drinking was only a small part of the problem since those who drank the most would usually pass out and were not capable of being abusive in such a state. He did not really know what to do about the problem of violence against women—this was a way of life for these men, and perhaps the women just needed to appreciate the support and protection they received from the king's warriors.

One woman who had her bones broken on more than one occasion found that just walking toward their family hut was a terrifying experience, and so one day after everyone had left the hut she set fire to it. That night she and her children slept in the hall of the woman, except for her older son, who slept with the other boys in the boy's hall. The only place for her husband to sleep was in the great hall, where he had to find a place to hide to be safe from Grendel. But Grendel did enter the hall that night and could indeed smell where the man was hiding, and took revenge. Though the community grieved this man's death, his wife was relieved. Though her sons no longer had a father to look up to, they did have an uncle, a brother of this woman, who took them under his wing and taught them what was expected of men. This uncle understood his sister's pain and was gentle with the boys, though their other uncle, the brother of the boys' father, held a resentment that diminished the bond between these two warriors.

This loss of morale caused Hrothgar to be concerned. When the next hut was burned down by another abused wife and the husband had to find a place to stay at night, the resentment of that wife by all the men grew, and now a new crisis was threatening to demoralize the entire community. Yet despite the censure of all the men, the abused wife felt her solution was better than the abuse she had suffered at the hands of her husband. The king found a partial solution by building a men's hall separate from the great hall, where the few single men could sleep in peace. Yet the problem of violence against women did not end, and the burning of huts by abused women did not end either, until the only solution the king could come up with was to encourage the men to sleep in the new man's hall and banish any woman who burned her hut. The latter part of this solution caused him great consternation but because of the coming of Grendel, he had no other options. He needed to keep his warriors safe to keep his kingdom safe.

Thus life was better for the women when their men would fall asleep in the new men's hall, or the great hall, Heorot, and not spend much time in their family hut. And as we know, the control and abuse of women would continue for the next two thousand years, though now there is some hope that this will end in this dawning of a new age.

22

FORSETASON REACHES VANADISDOTTIR

As we now know, two people can communicate with each other over a great distance through ecstatic trance, as did Baldr and Nanna in their relationship when Baldr lived in Asgard and Nanna lived in Vanaheim. Vanadisdottir knows that some priestesses are able to communicate this way, but so far she herself has not been successful in this particular ecstatic trance technique, though she has been successful in her nighttime dreams. I ask about this form of communication while in the Freyr Diviner posture, and I am given more information. Eventually this way of communicating will become most important as the tensions caused by Grendel's activities in Denmark mount . . .

Back in Scania for a visit, Forsetason settled down in his hut for the night. Later that night he had a dream. In his dream he stood with his knees bent and arms to his side as if he was about to jump.* As he stood in this ecstatic trance posture he saw Vanadisdottir lying on her sleeping platform in the hall of Queen Wealhtheow.

---

*This posture is seen in a figurine that was found in Højby, Denmark, from 300 to 500 CE; it is considered a middle world posture. It was introduced in Gunnar and Magnus Andersson's book (in Swedish) *Att föra gudarnas talan*, 77–78.

The Højby Middle World Posture

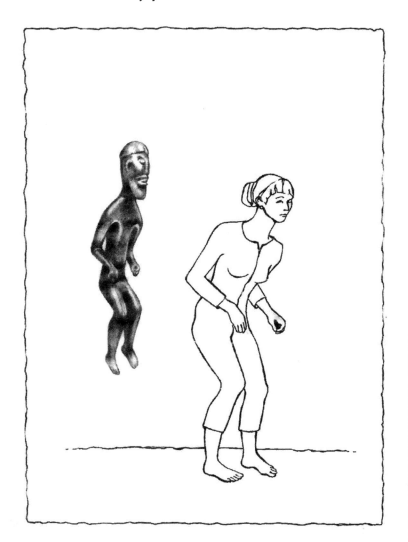

Stand with your feet parallel, toes pointing forward. Your arms are at your sides, elbows bent ninety degrees, your fingers curled. Lean your torso forward slightly and drop down slightly by bending your knees, as if you are about to jump. Find a comfortable position within this posture that you can hold for fifteen minutes.

He saw that along the wall at the priestess's feet was Gudvi's sleeping platform. Though Forsetason knew he was dreaming while he was in this dream, this time in seeing Vanadisdottir he wished she would wake up so they could talk to each other in the dream. While still dreaming, he saw his drum hanging from a post in his hut. While still in his dream he took the drum and held it low, along his waist, and started beating it rapidly to wake up Vanadisdottir. He realized that it would be very dark in the chamber in which she slept, yet in the dream he could see her clearly, as if in daylight. As he beat the drum he saw her open her eyes in her dream, and that she could see him, the same way that he, too, had his eyes open in his dream and could see her. Yet in reality both of them were still asleep and their eyes were closed.

He asked the priestess about what was going on in Hleidargard since the attack by Grendel, which he had seen vividly as he dreamed. She told him that Grendel continued to visit the great hall every few nights and told him about the abused wife who, fearing for her life, burned down her hut, and her husband who had been killed by Grendel the night he had to sleep in the great hall. Forsetason then told Vanadisdottir about his dream of seeing her, waking her with the drumming, and hearing her telling this story. In telling her this, he told her how he was standing—with his feet planted and his knees bent, as if he was about to leap forward, maybe all the way to Hleidargard. It was then that he saw her sleeping and wanted to wake her, so he took up his drum again and started beating. She smiled and told him that he had learned how to reach her in spirit travel. She reminded him that several years before she had told him that they could communicate without being together, and now he has learned something he can teach her. Before their time together in this dream ended, Forsetason told the priestess that he soon needed to visit her in person to validate for himself what had just happened in this dream.

The next morning, Forsetason, still feeling excited about this experience, knew he had to go to Hleidargard to talk to Vanadisdottir to prove to himself that what he had dreamed had indeed occurred, though he had no doubt that it was real. He went to Olaf to ask his permission to leave for a few days to visit Wealhtheow and Vanadisdottir. He was not yet ready to tell the king about Grendel's attacks and the killing until he proved to himself that his conversation with Vanadisdottir was real—specifically, that it was as real to her as it was to him.

Having gained the king's permission, Forsetason took his knapsack with those few things he would need for the short journey and walked the trail to the west harbor. He got there in the evening and bedded down for the night, knowing that the next day one of Olaf's ships would be crossing the strait to Hrothgar's east harbor to return some men to Hleidargard. The following day he would take one of these ships, which traveled the strait regularly, making traveling between Scania and Hleidargard easy.

Upon reaching Hleidargard, Forsetason first took the greetings of Olaf and his queen to Hrothgar and Wealhtheow. Wealhtheow was very pleased to see him. He told her about the health of her parents, that everything was well in Scania. He then sought out Vanadisdottir, who was not surprised to see him and had known he was on his way. He asked her how she knew, and she said that he had told her he was coming several nights ago. Then she told him everything that was said in their dreaming together.

As they talked, Forsetason asked Vanadisdottir if she could travel the same way to him, and she said that she didn't know if she could. Though she knew other priestesses who could do it, she had not perfected such journeying herself. She would occasionally have a lucid dream in which she knew she was dreaming and would ask questions or give directions to her dream, but she did not dream in this way a lot. Before Forsetason returned home he wanted her to try to connect with him in dreaming so that they both would know if she could do it again. He told her about waking in his dream and seeing her asleep. While dreaming he had stood with his knees bent and arms to his sides, as if he was preparing to jump across the strait to Hleidargard. In this position, to find a way to wake Vanadisdottir, he had taken his drum and held it low along his waist, beating it rapidly. So they made plans to do this very same thing again tonight. Vanadisdottir would sleep where she usually slept, in the hall of Wealhtheow. Forsetason would sleep where he preferred to sleep as a shepherd, in a simple shelter on a hill. At night the sheep were herded into their pen, and he then would return to the quiet of his shelter on the hill. At Hleidargard, the great hall was on the hill and the sheep grazed in the field below the hall to the north. There was no shelter there on the hill for the shepherd, so he built a simple lean-to where he would spend the night and try the dreaming experiment.

Later that night in the lean-to he awakened to hear someone or something coming toward him. It was Grendel. The creature was quiet and did not appear at all agitated as Vanadisdottir had described him in their earlier meeting. Forsetason motioned for Grendel to sit down near him, and he did. Grendel began to move his hands and arms in his own way to communicate, but Forsetason put his hand up to stop him, pointed to his own head, and then swept his hand down over his body to his place of harmony. Then he pointed to Grendel's head and swept his hand down in front of Grendel, pointing to the creature's place of harmony. After doing this several times he could tell that Grendel had moved to his place of harmony. They both smiled when Grendel began to hear the thoughts of Forsetason, and Forsetason knew what Grendel was thinking. He knew that other animals could read one another's minds in this way and that he himself was able to read the minds of animals, especially his sheep. He thought that Grendel's mind was closer to that of an animal than that of a human and therefore expected that they would be able to read each other's mind.

Grendel was thinking that he could trust the shepherd because he was a person of peace who cared for his sheep. And now he discovered that the shepherd even knew what his sheep were thinking. Forsetason nodded yes and told Grendel through his thoughts that he knew that Grendel was hungry and on his way to get a sheep from the king's pen, and that that was okay. Grendel said that he wanted to take it back to the cave he shared with his mother, to feed her, too, and that tonight he was not going into the great hall where the men were crazy, and that their craziness made him very angry.

As they sat together communicating in this way, Forsetason became aware of the presence of Vanadisdottir, who was being quiet so as not to disturb them. She was reaching him through dreaming. In the same way that he was communicating with Grendel, he communicated with the priestess, and the three of them started having a conversation. Vanadisdottir was curious about Grendel's mother and asked him how she was. He reported that she was strong and healthy but was getting old and rarely left their cave at the bottom of the dark pond. She depended on him to bring her food and watch over her. His father had died years ago, and he knew of no others of their kind, as they were the last ones of the old era. It was because of this that he hated to see the people of Hleidargard growing bigger and stronger in numbers and was jealous that they had one another and would last for a long time. Forsetason put his hand on Grendel's hand, showing him that he understood. With this, Forsetason went down to the sheep pen and brought back one of the sheep for Grendel.

The next day, before Forsetason left for home, he and Vanadisdottir talked about how they were unable to protect Grendel, and that eventually both Grendel and his mother would die. It would not be a great tragedy if their lives came to an early end at the hands of some great warrior—it would bring an end to their tragic lives as the last, lonely ones of their kind. But in the meantime, as opportunity might arise, they would be kind to Grendel and his mother and try to make their last years more comfortable.

23

A VISIT FROM BEOWULF

We already know a little about Beowulf as a result of Forsetason's visit to the land of the Geats. Forsetason believes that Beowulf is the answer to King Hrothgar's travails with Grendel. We know from the ancient story of Beowulf that after twelve years of torment Beowulf comes to rescue the king, and the twelfth year is now approaching. The question arises as to what is delaying his trip to Denmark, and how and what he knows about Grendel. The answers to my questions are again found in the Freyr Diviner posture. As the story continues, we learn why it is now so important for Vanadisdottir to be able to communicate from a distance . . .

This summer Prince Hrethric was twelve years old and received his first sword. Prince Hrothmund was nine, and Princess Freawaru was three. It has been nine years since Grendel first appeared. King Olaf and Queen Gunheid had not seen their grandchildren since the previous summer, so Queen Wealhtheow wanted to visit her parents in Scania. Hrothgar agreed to this and sent his brother, Halga, to escort the royal entourage. They left on the king's ship.

Vanadisdottir dreamed in order to send word to Foresetason that they would be arriving soon. The winds were right, so the royal party spent their first night in the east harbor. The next evening they arrived in Scania. Upon their arrival, Halga and his men set up the royal tent for Wealhtheow, Vanadisdottir, and the two boys and young princess.

The rest of the crew would find places in Olaf's hall to bed down for the duration of their visit. It was evening when their party arrived at the great hall of Olaf, so after greeting and dining with Olaf and Gunheid, Queen Wealhtheow, the priestess, and the children retreated to their tent.

The next day, after the queen, her mother, and the two younger children were settled and involved in their time together, Hrethric, now that he had his sword, wanted to watch Olaf's men on the practice field. Vanadisdottir asked permission to visit with Forsetason. She found him where she had expected sitting on the hillside with his sheep, the place where he felt most at peace. One of the sheep was lying contently at his side, being scratched behind the ears by the shepherd while he was watching a swallow building a nest in the roof of his lean-to. He seemed to understand animals and they trusted him. As the two of them talked, Vanadisdottir told stories of the demise of the many champions of King Hrothgar at the hands of Grendel, as well as the demise of many of the chieftains of the northern lands who thought they might be able to rid King Hrothgar of his tormenter. As they talked, Forsetason thought of the Geat king Hygelac's nephew and champion, the powerful hero Beowulf. Beowulf might be the answer to the Danes' problem. This massive warrior had won every battle and competition he had ever entered. At the mention of King Hygelac, Vanadisdottir recalled that a traveling merchant who had once stopped at Hleidargard had told her about a priestess of Freyja who now resided among the Geats. She wondered if she could send word to this priestess through dreaming, in the same way that she and Forsetason had been able to communicate from a distance, and just as Nanna and Baldr did.

That night she went to sleep with the intention of dreaming of her sister priestess who lived among the Geats. In a dream in the early morning hours she saw this priestess lying on her sleeping platform, and in her dream Vanadisdottir stood to beat her drum to get the priestess's attention. As she did so she saw the priestess open her eyes and they greeted each other. After catching up on the news of what each priestess had been doing with her life since leaving the tarn of Freyja, Vanadisdottir told her of Hrothgar's travails, and she asked after Beowulf. The Geat priestess told her that he was now traveling in the domain of King Athils. King Hygelac had thought it would be beneficial to both him and King Athils for them to make peace. Though by ship their kingdoms were a great distance apart, on opposite sides of Sweden, by land the borders of their kingdoms almost touched, with only a narrow strip of outlawry between them. If peace were made and an alliance formed, this outlaw zone could be divided between them, and they might be better able to protect the people whose farmsteads were close to the border. Thus the king had sent Beowulf on this mission to Athils. Rather than traveling by ship around Sweden, Beowulf preferred to journey by horseback across the land. He reasoned that arriving by ship might be perceived as more of a threat than arriving alone at Uppsala. Hygelac was neither a Skjǫldung nor an Yngling, but rather had his own center for the worship of the gods in the land of the Geats, at Tanum; the Geat king was considered neutral in the rivalry between these two competing royal families. Thus this was King Hygelac's hope, and he did not expect to see his champion return for a year while on this mission.

Queen Wealhtheow's entourage did not leave Scania for another two days. On the way home they were delayed for a couple of days at Hrothgar's east harbor because of a nighttime attack by warrior ships from Norway. The king of Norway resented the patrolling of the strait and having to pay a toll to Hrothgar to pass. He had sent three ships to attack them at the east harbor; however, the Norwegian king was not aware of the powers of Forsetason to see the impending attack in his dreaming. As he dreamed of the attack, Forsetason reached out to Vanadisdottir in his dreaming to warn her and the others at the east harbor. The priestess immediately awakened from her dream and ran to warn Halga about the imminent attack.

Because the nights were short at this time of the year, Halga did not have much time to prepare before the early-dawn attack, but he did have time to prepare an ambush. As the Norwegian warriors arrived, the settlement was quiet, and the people at the harbor appeared to be still sleeping or just waking. The queen, Vanadisdottir, and the three boys were placed in a small boat and taken to safety through the marsh, to the west of the small settlement. The forty men of Hrothgar quietly hid in the woods to the north of the settlement while the men from two of the Norwegian ships disembarked and came ashore. The third ship remained a short distance from shore in case ships from the west harbor appeared. While approaching the east harbor they had seen a sentry fire burning across the strait, and they knew it was carrying a message to the other harbor. By the time they came ashore, the signal fire in the west harbor was burning, too. This fire indicated to the invaders that Hrothgar's men must still be in the settlement and did not expect them to be hiding in the woods, so they were surprised when Halga's men came forward in a tight wedge formation. The battle that ensued was fierce, and Hrothgar lost a few men, but in the end most of the Norwegians lay dead, and the third ship left, heading back north, pursued by two ships from the west harbor.

Following the morning attack, the subsequent journey home by Wealhtheow and her children and companions was uneventful, though they did pass the burning Norwegian ship before they rounded the northern tip of Denmark.

Later that fall a merchant ship bearing Beowulf came into Olaf's harbor at Scania. Though Forsetason did not ordinarily spend much time in Olaf's hall, preferring his hut on the hill and his solitude, he followed Beowulf into the hall and sat to one side, where he could listen to the conversation between Beowulf and Olaf. Other men were also in the hall, as such conversations were not held in private. Beowulf told Olaf of the nature of his journey and of the time he had spent with Athils. There he had been challenged in various competitions by Athils's champions, and he had gained Athils's respect by prevailing in all challenges. During his time at Uppsala Beowulf had learned a lot about this Yngling king, and though Beowulf had gained the king's respect and

Athils now talked about making peace, Beowulf knew he could not be trusted, that he was very greedy and always looking for a way he could take advantage of others. Though Hygelac thought Beowulf might stay in the realm of Athils for the winter, Beowulf, not trusting the king, left when he had the opportunity to join this merchant ship's crew. He never minded being an oarsman on a ship and regarded rowing as a relaxing experience.

As Beowulf and the king talked, the warrior glimpsed Forsetason and recognized him, for who could not remember that face? He then told Olaf how much he had enjoyed the time he had spent with Bragason and Forsetason, and of the stories they had told in the court of Hygelac. Beowulf was in a hurry to get back to Hygelac before winter set in, and the merchant assured him that that was to be his next stop after spending a couple of days trading in Scania. Though throughout the north any king might be at war with any other, traveling merchants, regardless of their country of origin, were always accepted with open arms.

When Beowulf left the hall that afternoon Forsetason left with him, and the two of them found a place to sit and talk. Beowulf knew of Hrothgar's travails and was interested in Forsetason's knowledge of Grendel. The warrior needed to return to Hygelac at this time but had thought of assisting Hrothgar the following summer. Forsetason told him that no weapon could penetrate Grendel's hide and that his claws could cut anything as if it were a thin leaf. He told of how Grendel drank the blood of men and sliced open their legs and took the sinew to chew, taking a leg or two torn from the warriors' bodies with him back to his cave at the bottom of a lake. Hearing this, Beowulf knew his only chance would be to grab Grendel's arms and not let go, because it was with his arms that he killed. Forsetason agreed that his idea was the only way of ridding Hrothgar of this creature. Forsetason also told Beowulf to pay attention to the news that might come from the priestess of Freyja who lived with the Geats—that Queen Wealhtheow's priestess, Vanadisdottir, and this priestess were able to dream together and in this way communicate back and forth. In this way Beowulf could get the latest news about Grendel.

After two days of trading, feasting, and celebration, Beowulf left on the merchant ship to return to the land of the Geats. Upon arriving home, Beowulf told Hygelac about Grendel and the humiliation he had caused their friend King Hrothgar. He told his king of his intention of rescuing Hrothgar from further humiliation. Hygelac was in favor of Beowulf's plan because he was always seeking ways to form alliances for greater strength and to bring peace to the north. In this way Hrothgar and Hygelac were of the same mind in wanting peace. Vanadisdottir learned of Hygelac's feelings because the Geat priestess of Freyja was in the king's hall at the time he met with Beowulf, and she subsequently related the meeting to Vanadisdottir in her dreaming. The two priestesses were enjoying this newfound way of communicating and used it every chance they could.

24

THE ELEVENTH YEAR

Vanadisdottir's role among the Danes as priestess and healer expands. She has made many friends and converts to her beliefs concerning the Great Mother. At this time she takes under her wing a certain young boy, Healfdall, who does not want to be a warrior but prefers instead to sit on the hillside with the sheep. She first teaches him to see as she first taught Forsetason. In asking what happens next in this unfolding saga, the spirit of Freyr reveals to me the importance of seeing and the recognition by a few more people that the spirit of the creature Grendel is actually quite gentle. Also, my original question about how nurturing women dealt with men of violence at this time is further illuminated when, sitting in the Freyr Diviner posture, I am shown how some women in the settlement come to Vanadisdottir because they worry about their sons choosing to become warriors . . .

Because of Grendel's continual torment of the warriors of King Hrothgar, no one slept in Heorot anymore, and there were those who missed the comforts and warmth of sleeping in the great hall. Grendel had not been seen for some time except for occasional reports from farmers in the outlying areas of the king's land, who would find a sheep missing in the morning and come across the creature's footprints. It was apparent that Grendel did not want the farmer families to suffer, so he would take only one sheep and then quietly leave. He would likely not return to that particular farm for over a year, so the loss of one sheep was no major loss to the family. Grendel apparently was skilled in hunting other animals for food, especially deer and wild pigs, and he generally left the common folk alone.

Yet the greatest and strongest king in the north had been humiliated by the torment inflicted on him by Grendel, and so Hrothgar continued to try to find ways to rid himself of the monster. There had been talk of Beowulf, the strongest of men and champion of King Hygelac, being his only hope, and the rumor had gone around that the warrior might come to the king's rescue later that summer. The king had heard this rumor from his queen, who heard it from Vanadisdottir. When Beowulf did not arrive, Vanadisdottir used her skill of communicating at a distance through drumming and dreaming to reach out to the priestess of Freyja who lived among the Geats, to learn of Beowulf's plans. In this way she learned that Hygelac was battling the king of Norway and needed Beowulf, and thus Beowulf's original plan had changed.

Vanadisdottir was always eager to teach others the ways of seiðr. Remember the story of Healfdall who did not want to be a warrior and spent his time sitting on the hillside with his young friend who tended the sheep, the two boys who were being taught the ways of seiðr by Vanadisdottir? Remember how he used his power of seeing to find his father who lay unconscious in a ravine after being gored by a boar? His story now continues. He told no one at first, but when he stopped and sat to beat his drum in the place where his father was last seen, he had the vision of his father in the ravine but also saw in his vision a shimmering image of something else that was unclear to him. He did not understand, nor was he sure of what he saw, and being most concerned about his father, he did not think of the rest of his vision for a couple of days. Then he went back to the place and again sat and beat his drum and the vision came back to him. He saw a shimmering image of something that appeared to be what he thought was Grendel, but the monster was kneeling beside his father, gently caressing his head. By the time he had reached his father's side, Grendel was gone.

He did not think he could believe his vision, but then he told

Vanadisdottir what he saw. She smiled and told him about her meetings with Grendel. She told Healfdall about this tender side of Grendel, and how he took care of his mother, the last woman of their kind. "His kind led a different life. They took from the earth only what they needed to live and valued the earth for what it provided. Grendel, the last of this breed, values the earth, but disdains those who fight, those who seek wealth and power to control the earth. He sees them as destroying the peaceful life into which he was born. That's why he doesn't bother the farmers and their families, because he sees them appreciating the earth. He came to me when he saw that I was in harmony with the animals and that the animals trusted me. He knew he could trust me, and he could trust Forsetason, who saw him too. He could trust King Healfdene, King Hrothgar's father and your namesake, who in the last days of his life discovered his center of harmony so that the deer and ravens would come to him. Though the king had not seen Grendel, Grendel had watched him feeding the deer and birds and grieved his death. I am sure Grendel has watched you and knows he can trust you. Coming from the era of the Great Mother, he looks longingly at those he sees caring for the animals and the earth and feels very lonely at this time because there are so few he can trust."

Hearing this, Healfdall, in his own way of journeying, used a shape-shifting posture, sitting with his legs crossed, imagining himself as a four-legged animal while he drummed.* In this way he could see as though he was seeing through the eyes of Grendel. He could feel the feelings of Grendel, feel his compassion for the simple farmers and others who show their respect for Mother Earth and their gratitude for how she provides and cares for her beings. He could feel Grendel's anger whenever he saw men fighting, drinking, abusing women, and taking everything they could from Mother Earth. He also felt Grendel's pain and the loneliness of being the last of his kind.

---

*Healfdall sat in the Olmec Prince posture. More on this posture can be found in *The Power of Ecstatic Trance.*

Outside of the torment by Grendel, battles were rare now because of the many alliances made by King Healfdene and his successor, King Hrothgar. There were also fewer raiders and outlaws. As for any chieftain who still resisted Hrothgar, few were willing to fight him. In this way Hrothgar had brought a greater level of peace to the land, though his men still needed to practice constantly and challenge one another to retain their position of strength.

During this time Wealhtheow continued to listen to the stories of the women of the settlement, and in particular one mother, Liknvi, who had lost a son in a battle with raiders along the strait between Gefjon's island and Scania. The death of this mother's son still haunted Wealhtheow, and the mother feared that her second son would soon become a warrior. She herself had grown up a farmer's daughter, and though she had bettered her life by marrying a warrior, she now was remembering and valuing the life of the farmer and wished her next son would return to that life.

Wealhtheow told Liknvi, the story of Griðbustaðr, the Dwelling Place of Peace, where those who understand and practice the compassionate magic of the Vanir reside after death. Liknvi did not know about Griðbustaðr. She knew only about Valhalla, where warriors who die in battle go after death, and Hel, where those who die of illness and old age go. She also knew that Freyja took some of the warriors to Gæfuleysabjarg, the Cliff of Lucklessness, but she did not know that those she took there were warriors who died in their first battle. As well, she knew that Gefjon took those women who died as virgins to Gratabjǫð, the Weeping Fields, but she did not know that Gratabjǫð was separated from Gæfuleysabjarg by the deep gorge Harmagil, from which the smell of sulfur rose from the underworld hall of Hel. In hearing about all of this she came to the conclusion that her first son must be on the Cliff of Lucklessness.

Wealhtheow continued: "Those who die and who find their way to Griðbustaðr will find peace and contentment. What prevents warriors from going there is their continued value of strength and valor in battle, their valuing of armor and weaponry over all else. Those who died in their first battle are separated from the women who died as virgins by Harmagil, the deep gorge. They can see these virgins and spend their time flexing their muscles and showing off their strength in their attempt to impress these young women. Or they can find their way to Griðbustaðr by using the ways of seiðr, but to do so they have to end their ways of trying to impress others through physical strength and learn to value contentment and being at one with the earth. Most don't make this leap in understanding. Baldr, the most beautiful and gentle son of Odin and Frigg, has journeyed to Gæfuleysabjarg and has listened patiently and gently to the stories of these fallen warriors, and in this way he has demonstrated to them the power of gentleness and harmony. The warriors love Baldr for his ability to listen, but most of them do not understand his ways unless they were lucky enough in their youth to learn and understand the ways of seiðr. In the same way, the virgins have also missed the opportunity to journey to Griðbustaðr because they are so fragile and impressed by these warrior's antics. I hope someday everyone will value and practice seiðr—that is why I teach it whenever I find someone willing to listen."

The princess Signy was present while Wealhtheow was speaking about the afterlife to Liknvi and the conversation had caught her attention. Signy was quite concerned about her own son Hrok, who by now was old enough to fight alongside Hrothgar's warriors. He had recently received a minor wound on his leg that was treated successfully by Vanadisdottir and was now back practicing his warrior skills. Upon hearing what Wealhtheow had just told them, Signy and Liknvi wanted to learn more, and Wealhtheow told them they needed to consult with Vanadisdottir.

The priestess informed the two women that they were already well on their way to understanding seiðr because they questioned the warrior values—at least as far as their sons were concerned. They were the kind of women who appreciated learning about what the Great

Mother has to offer in the form of plants and herbs that heal and provide other benefits for a healthy life. Both women understood the power of their center of harmony for learning about plants, and they had seen how a few of the young boys could call animals to them by moving their attention to their center of harmony. Vanadisdottir told them about the many other uses of the center of harmony, and of the ability to stalk like a cat in order to learn about Mother Earth and what she provides.

In particular, Signy and Liknvi were most eager to learn about how to journey to Griðbustaðr, but Vanadisdottir felt that they needed to first learn one other thing—the power of seeing through the eyes of another. By learning how to do this they could then learn to see through the eyes of the dead in order to see Griðbustaðr. She explained to the women that this takes using a metamorphosis posture for spirit journeying, a posture that would allow them to become one with something else, like becoming a deer or a sheep. Both Vanadisdottir and the two women found a quiet place for their ecstatic journey, and after calling to the spirits of the animals, they sat on the ground with their legs crossed in front of them, while holding over their heads branches that looked like the antlers of a deer.*

In this posture, while the women's eyes were closed, the priestess laid her own antlers on the ground and began beating her drum rapidly. After some time she brought her drumming to an end and asked Signy and Liknvi what they had experienced. Liknvi reported that she felt like she was walking through the woods on four legs. She stopped by certain trees and nibbled on the leaves of those trees. She then heard a noise and saw a man, so she turned and ran deeper into the woods. She had seen through the eyes of a deer. Signy's experience was similar: she reported that as a deer she ran through the woods, pursued by a hunter. She felt a spear brush her side, but she was too fast and got away.

---

*This posture, the Cernunnos Metamorphosis posture, was found in Denmark and is described by Gore in *Ecstatic Experience,* 91–94.

The Cernunnos Metamorphosis Posture

Sit on the floor with your legs crossed in front of you. Bring your right calf as close to your right thigh as possible, so that your foot rests in front of your crotch. Position your left leg so that the calf rests in front of your right leg. With your shoulders squared, hold your arms to the side of your body and bend your elbows so that your hands are at shoulder level, creating a *V* shape with each arm. Face forward, with your eyes and mouth slightly open, as though you were preparing to whistle. Optional: wear a pair of horns on your head and hold a snake in your left hand and a torque in your right.

The next day Vanadisdottir repeated this trance journey, but this time she asked the two mothers to think of their grandmothers. Liknvi's grandmother had died when she was young. Signy's had been the consort of King Beow who died many years earlier. The two women were asked to think of some question they would like to ask their grandmother. She then had Signy and Liknvi lie down on the ground with their arms to their sides and their left knees comfortably raised.*

When the drumming stopped, both women gasped in horror at what Niflheim, the realm of those who die of illness and old age, is like. Liknvi reported seeing her grandmother looking like not much more than a skeleton, just sitting in that damp, dark place that stank of sulfur. She asked her grandmother about her son, Likvi's father, who had died several years ago. The grandmother nodded with her head to her right, and there, a few feet away, sat Liknvi's father, also looking like a skeleton, dripping wet in this damp underworld. Though Signy's grandmother had been a queen, Signy had found her in Niflheim, too. She asked her grandmother what she knew about the old ways, about seiðr, and her grandmother told her that she had to be faithful to her husband, who did not believe in the old ways, so she always remained at his side in his beliefs in Odin and Thor.

The next time Signy and Liknvi got together to learn in this quiet and special place with Vanadisdottir, Wealhtheow and two other women joined them. Since Vanadisdottir was her guvernante, Wealhtheow had been practicing these ways of seiðr since she was quite young and always enjoyed going on ecstatic journeys. The other two women who came with Wealtheow had become part of the group a year or two before for reasons not much different from Liknvi's.

---

*This posture was found in the petroglyphs of Tanum, Sweden, and is called the Tanum Lower World posture. You can see this image in Coles, *Shadows of the Norther Past,* 136.

The Tanum Lower World Posture

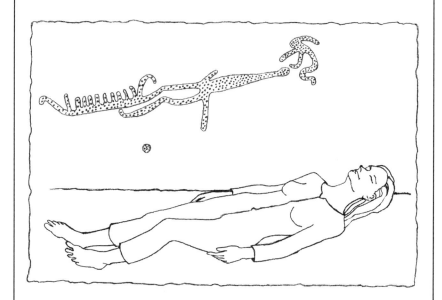

Lie on your back with your arms at your sides, close to your body. Your legs are essentially parallel, though your left knee may be slightly raised.

For this journey, Vanadisdottir had all the women bring their sleeping platforms and showed them how to set them up. She first pounded two short but strong branches or pegs into the ground at the foot of the platform. She then took another longer branch and marked a line in the dirt that was four lengths of this branch up from the foot of the platform. She then found some strong branches that were a little longer than three lengths of her measuring branch and pounded the ends of these branches into the ground on the line she had drawn, so that they stood straight up, three lengths above the ground, such that they would hold the head of the sleeping platform higher than the foot of the platform, which was resting on the shorter pegs. When each of the five women had set up their sleeping platforms in this way and were lying on their platforms with their heads raised above their feet, Vanadisdottir told them that during ancient times when a body was placed on a funeral pyre it was placed at this angle, with the head up so that it would rise to Griðbustaðr.* With the body in this position, the smoke could be seen as rising from the fire and out of the head of the body.

Vanadisdottir called on the more distant ancestors of these women to be with them, ancestors who lived at the time when the people worshipped the Great Mother and Freyja. She suggested that these distant ancestors could lead these women on this spirit journey. Then she began beating her drum rapidly. While in this posture, the women journeyed to Griðbustaðr, a beautiful and sunny place where those who have died live in peace and contentment, working together to make the lives of all pleasant and comfortable.

This group of women subsequently met regularly with Vanadisdottir and learned about the powers of ecstatic trance. As time went by, a few more women joined this small but growing group learning the ways of seiðr. Liknvi tried to tell her son about her experiences, and though he listened to her she was not sure what his thoughts were about what she had told him, and so she did not think he was ready

---

*Over the last year I have been having moments when I see a peripheral shimmer in my visual field, a kind of aura similar to what people experience before a migraine headache, though for me I do not have this kind of intense headache. One morning a week or so ago I had a nighttime dream that these visual experiences indicated that there was some message awaiting me in ecstatic trance and that the next time I had such an experience I needed to go into trance. That happened on August 30, 2013, and my trance experience using the divination posture first took me to the petroglyphs of Tanum, and then further back in time, to a funeral pyre where the body was laying at a 37-degree angle. I watched the smoke rising from under the platform. The smoke was deflected by the platform at a 37-degree angle and flowed upward, as if out of the head of the body. By that date in August a first draft of this manuscript was almost finished and I returned to this chapter to add this observation.

to learn about Griðbustaðr. He still dreamed about someday going to Valhalla. Hrok, Signy's son, was learning how to fight, but he sometimes went out with his father while his father collected tribute from the chieftains. Hrok knew that being a strong warrior was important, but as a result of his travels with his father he was also learning about the value of negotiating with others without fighting, and so he was beginning to have thoughts about becoming a counselor to the king instead of a warrior.

Thus the eleventh year after the coming of Grendel passed.

25

THE END OF GRENDEL

This part of the story is well known from the oldest poem known in the English language, *Beowulf*, so there is not much to ask about what happens next in the saga. The only question I have concerns how Vanadisdottir deals with her knowledge of Grendel's gentle side as his death approaches. The answer comes in ecstatic trance using the Freyr Diviner posture, where I see her withdrawing from the others, at the edge of the pond near the great hall, offering the mother of Grendel her sympathy, and later reaching out to Forsetason to tell him what happened. For those of you who have read the ancient epic poem *Beowulf*, you know what happens next . . .

After twelve years of Grendel's unrelenting torment, the strongest of living men, the Geat warrior Beowulf, arrived in the realm of King Hrothgar. The sentry watched the flag-bedecked ship carrying Beowulf and fourteen hand-picked men, the bravest of King Hygelac's warriors, as it pulled into the harbor at Hleidargard. The warriors carried shields and swords, spears and axes. No war party had ever entered this kingdom so boldly.

As they disembarked, the sentry questioned them as to the purpose of their visit, and Beowulf replied that they had come with the purpose of ridding King Hrothgar of his murderous foe. The sentry promised safe harbor for the ship and provided Beowulf and his warriors with a guide to lead them up to the king's great hall. The warriors sported glittering armor and armbands that signified bravery. Arriving at the great hall, they laid their weapons down against the wall outside the great hall of the king. Wulfgar, a retainer in Hrothgar's court, listened to Beowulf as he recited his lineage and announced that he and his party of warriors had come in friendship, as allies. Wulfgar then led the visitors into the great hall to stand before the king's high seat, where Beowulf identified himself as the son of the famous Ecgtheow, a "noble battle-leader" and champion of King Hygelac. Hrothgar acknowledged that he knew Beowulf when he was just a lad, and expressed his certainty that the gods had sent him to help the Danes. The king and Beowulf then commenced to share stories of their knowledge of each other. In this manner Beowulf was warmly welcomed.

One story told was of Beowulf's swimming race with Breca across the northern seas. Hearing this, Unferth, who sat in a place of honor among Hrothgar's men, expressed with a faint tinge of jealousy his belief that Beowulf had lost the race, but Beowulf quickly corrected him in a convincing manner with the facts: that he had swum much farther than Breca, to the shores of the Finns. He further regaled them with tales of how he had battled sea monsters as he swam.

Queen Wealhtheow, adorned in gold, came into the hall, as it was customary to greet important visitors to the kingdom. She offered Beowulf a goblet from which to drink, after which everyone in the hall commenced eating, drinking, and general revelry. Though Grendel did not come into the great hall every single night since he now knew that men seldom slept there anymore, such revelry in the hall was a clearly intended invitation to him to come on this particular night. The festivities resounded in the hall until Hrothgar, with his queen, Wealhtheow, accompanied by a band of his retainers, left to go to their respective places to sleep. The confident leader of the Geats, along with his fourteen men, remained to guard the great hall.

Beowulf took off his armor and gave it, along with his sword, to a servant to care for as he prepared for sleep. He then proclaimed to his men that his armor and weapons would be useless in dispensing with a monster that has no knowledge of such weapons, so he would rely solely on his sheer physical strength. The men from the realm of King Hygelac then settled in for the night, with Beowulf, a berserker, lying naked on the floor of the king's banquet hall, where he allowed himself to feel his furious strength welling up. His men fell asleep while Beowulf kept watch on this, the blackest of nights.

After a short while, the Geat champion heard the heavy footfalls of the stalking monster coming from the direction of the moors, approaching Heorot. Though the doors of the great hall were secured with an iron bar, they burst open at the slightest push by the creature, who then entered. Beowulf observed the methods of Grendel as the creature reached for and snatched the first sleeping man, tore him apart, and drank his blood before swallowing his flesh. As Grendel advanced toward Beowulf and made ready to grab him, the Geat hero sprang up and grabbed hold of Grendel's arm, but missed grabbing the second arm as well. He had to move fast before Grendel used his one free arm to slice Beowulf open. He twisted the monster's arm with all of his strength and heard the sinew of Grendel's shoulder snap with a loud pop. He then was free to grab the monster's other arm with both hands. The struggle continued with increased intensity. The monster dragged Beowulf around the room, wreaking havoc inside the great hall, but throughout the titanic struggle Beowulf did not let go. The warrior twisted the monster's other arm until he heard the sinew snapping. Still hanging on to life, Grendel fought to escape the great hall, the flesh of his arm now separated from his body, and he made his way out with one less arm, the other hanging limply at his side, as the remaining warriors trailed him.

Outside, the battle in the hall had awakened every single Dane. The howling creature of a previous era headed toward his lair at the bottom of the lake, trailed by Beowulf's men. They struck Grendel with swords and spears, but nothing would penetrate the monster's tough hide, and Grendel escaped. Yet the victory was Beowulf's, as the tearing off of the monster's arms fulfilled the wish of every Dane.

As dawn broke, the Danes gathered in what remained of Heorot to see the massive, taloned arm of Grendel. One of the men took the arm, climbed to the gable above what had been the entrance to the great hall, and hung it there for all to see. The fiend's trail of blood was clear; the men followed it through the moors that led down to the lake, where they found the water red with the monster's blood. Then everyone returned to the hall. As Hrothgar entered and saw the arm hanging above the door, he rejoiced and gave thanks. Peace had finally come to him and the Danish people. The king proclaimed that hereafter Beowulf was his son, and that the hero would never be lacking in worldly goods and wealth. Beowulf replied that he regreted that Grendel had escaped his grasp when he had hoped to have the monster's entire body as proof of his final victory, though everyone knew that with the grave wounds the creature had sustained, his death was certainly not far off. Quietly, in his own way, Beowulf gave credit to Forsetason, who had given him the knowledge that led to this victory.

Meanwhile, Vanadisdottir, hearing Beowulf's expressions of victory, retreated to the edge of the pond, not far from the one cave entrance she knew led to Grendel's lair. From there she was able to reach Forsetason in Scania through their way of dreaming together to let her protégé know what had happened. Together in their dreaming trance they expressed their condolences to the mother of Grendel, who they knew grieved in her den beneath the lake. Upon returning to the hall Vanadisdottir found Wealhtheow and Beowulf together and she let them know that she had told Forsetason about the victory, for only they knew about and believed in the power of dreaming. In their dreaming together Forsetason had told the priestess that the people of Olaf's realm were celebrating Beowulf's victory too.

A large group of Danes was needed to repair and redecorate the great hall with golden tapestries in preparation for an evening of celebration and feasting, with many toasts of mead. Beowulf received ample rewards in the form of gold and jewels from the king. Many stories were told and ballads sung about the strongest hero of the north, as

Beowulf sat in the place of honor between Prince Hrethric and Prince Hrothmund, the two natural-born sons of King Hrothgar and Queen Wealhtheow. Beowulf would now and forever after be regarded as one of the sons of the king and queen.

Prince Hrothmund, now twelve years old, sat proudly with his new sword adorning the table before him. Beowulf praised the sword and told him of his own first sword and his first heroic act. He related how he had stood near a hut where a woman had been hanging clothing to dry when a lost and confused boar charged her. As she ran around the corner of her hut with the boar in pursuit, Beowulf thrust his sword into the flank of the boar, killing it. Hearing this story, Hrothmund told Beowulf of his Uncle Olfdene, his mother's brother whom he had never met, who killed his best friend in a rage for having killed his dog. Because of this, the uncle had been banished to England, where he fought with Æðelstan and died in battle alongside his Uncle Heorogar, his father's brother and heir to the throne in which his own father now sat. Because of this story, which had been told him by his mother, Wealhtheow, he knew of the importance of controlling one's anger when in battle, because anger only clouds one's thinking and causes the person to make mistakes.

The men celebrated late into the night and finally the benches were cleared away and bedding spread out so that the men could bed down before the sun rose, as had once been the custom before the coming of Grendel. And so they bedded down in their great hall, where they had not felt free for twelve years, and they slept in peace. Beowulf was given special quarters in which to sleep, quarters saved for special guests of the king. Thus a peaceful silence fell over the Danish kingdom at long last.

26

THE MOTHER OF GRENDEL

Following the night of celebration, we know from the epic poem *Beowulf* how Grendel's mother came into the great hall, and about the battle between this she-monster and Beowulf. There is not much more to add to this saga other than what is seen in my vision when I ask the spirit of Freyja about Vanadisdottir, who realizes that the misery of these last two creatures of another era is now over . . .

As the men slept soundly in the great hall, revenge, in the form of Grendel's mother, stalked the outside world. A she-beast, the mother of Grendel came from the fens that lay to the east of Heorot, where Vanadisdottir sat the day before as she communed with Forsetason. The mother, not quite as strong as her son but still formidable, was able to break down the hall's door and enter. She did not know what to expect, and as the men awakened and jumped up, grabbing their swords, she snatched one man near the door, a most beloved chieftain to Hrothgar, and, carrying him, left in haste, taking with her the taloned arm of her son, which she found hanging above the portal. A familiar gloom returned to the hall; Hrothgar was heartbroken. Beowulf was called and came before the king, not knowing what had happened. Hearing of the loss of Hrothgar's closest counselor, Beowulf was again challenged by the king to finish the job, by killing Grendel's mother.

Beowulf once again called together his men, and they followed the she-monster's tracks to the dark lake overhung with trees and roots. Hanging above the lake, impaled on the branch of a tree, was the head of Beowulf's trusted counselor. Peering into the lake, the warriors could see many sea monsters, reptiles, and serpents. Beowulf wore his helmet and armor and carried his shield. He asked Hrothgar to watch over his retainers should he not return. He then dove into the depths of the lake with his sword and spear, dispatching the sea creatures one after another as he plunged deeper toward the bottom. Though it took him the better part of the day to reach the bottom, it was not long before the mother of Grendel realized that someone was coming toward her lair.

When she saw Beowulf she lunged and grabbed him with her talons, but his armor protected him from injury. She carried him into her den, where he found there was air to breathe. In the fire-lit cave he could now see his enemy. With a powerful swing of his sword he struck the neck of the sea-hag, but his weapon recoiled off her hide, leaving her uninjured. From then on it was hand-to-hand combat as Beowulf flung her to the floor. Rising, she seized him again. Weakened, the hero stumbled and fell to the floor. In the course of their struggle he could see in the cave a famous sword forged by the giants, too large and heavy for most men to lift. Yet in the fighting frenzy of a true berserker, Beowulf grabbed the sword and swung it mightily, catching the monster on her neck, severing her head cleanly from her body.

Above, at the edge of the lake, the men waited and watched nervously as the lake boiled with blood. After nine hours, Hrothgar and his men assumed that Beowulf was dead and dismally left to return to Heorot, but Beowulf's men remained, hoping their hero would emerge.

The fiery blood of the mother of Grendel had melted the blade of the sword that Beowulf had used to decapitate her. Inside the cave, Beowulf could see the remains of Grendel. Though the lair was strewn with treasure, he touched none of it, but rather only the head of Grendel and the hilt of the blood-dissolved sword. These he carried with him as he swam to the surface of the lake, now purified by the death of its denizens. Bobbing to the surface, Beowulf's men rejoiced. Because of the enormous size of Grendel's head, four men were needed to carry it back to the great hall.

The men entered the hall with this fearful spectacle, both a trophy and proof of Beowulf's victory. This they paraded in front of the king and queen. Beowulf then regaled all those present with his story of the final battle, of nearly losing his life. In the end his victory over Grendel's mother brought him satisfaction because it finally brought peace to the king and queen and the Danish people. He offered the king the golden, jewel-encrusted hilt of the famous sword that had brought an end to the she-monster and explained that her blood had dissolved its blade. The celebrating continued well into the night, with the king rewarding Beowulf with yet more treasure. More speeches were made and songs sung, proclaiming the victory.

Hrothgar was now approaching his fiftieth year, the last twenty of which he had reigned as king. Most important to him were the values other than strength and courage that were demonstrated by Beowulf—humility and benevolence—values that had made Hrothgar the greatest king of Denmark. The king believed that greed was the driving force behind some kings' evil deeds and would lead only to their eventual destruction. Hrothgar's generosity in giving away armbands and treasure to those who showed valor and loyalty without actually seeking recognition or wealth revealed his wisdom and brought many great warriors to his realm to become his retainers, and other leaders to his side. His relationships with two leaders in particular were special in this regard—King Hygelac of the Geats, and High Chief Olaf of Scania.

Finally, Hrothgar bid the assembly good night and retired to the hall of the queen, as others similarly retired to their own places to find comfort and peace in a well-earned sleep.

During all of the chaos of the day, no one had paid any attention to Vanadisdottir except the queen. The previous night, at around the same time the mother of Grendel had entered Heorot, Forsetason again saw what was happening in his dream. He then dreamed with intent, sending his vision to Vanadisdottir. Though it was too late for the priestess to warn the men who slept in the hall, Forsetason sent Vanadisdottir his vision of seeing Beowulf in the cave at the bottom of the boiling lake, and the great struggle between Beowulf and Grendel's mother, with the Geat's victory in slaying her with the sword of the giants. This vision Vanadisdottir shared with Wealhtheow. And when the king returned without Beowulf to say that he thought the Geat champion must be dead, Wealhtheow assured him that was not the case—that the Geat lived and was victorious. And so when Beowulf returned to Heorot with the hilt of the giant's great sword and the head of Grendel, Hrothgar was not greatly surprised, and his trust in the dreaming powers of Vanadisdottir and Forsetason grew even stronger.

The next day, the Geat warrior expressed his intention to return to his home and to King Hygelac. He told King Hrothgar that he would always be ready to come to his aid, and that he and his family would always have plenty of friends in the court of the Geat king. Hrothgar, with Queen Wealhtheow at his side, told Beowulf that he expected Beowulf to become king after the end of Hygelac's reign, and that he believed he would bring peace to the people of the north. Feuds and wars between the kings and chieftains must come to an end, the king declared.

Well over a thousand years later, as we now know, the dream of this ancient king has yet to come true, though it continues to be the dream of many. Now as then, feuds and war continue to rage around the world because of the evil of greed. In his continued dream of peace among the people of the north, King Hrothgar, in his later years, would offer his daughter Freawaru in marriage to Prince Ingeld, the son of the Heathobard king, Froda, in the hope that the union would bring to an end the longlasting feud between these two kingdoms. But unfortunately the spears would not long lie idle . . .

At dawn the next morning, Beowulf and his men loaded their ship with their treasure of gold and horses and set off for home across the sea. As they approached the land of the Geats, the magnificent hall of

King Hygelac came into view, standing high atop a cliff overlooking the sea. Beowulf gladly brought the gold and horses he had received from his venture in the realm of Hrothgar to the feet of his king and queen, who ceremoniously greeted their returning hero and his men and offered a night of gaiety and feasting, with Beowulf again sharing his story of success and of making new friends with their fellows to the south.

In later years, as a result of the misfortunate war with the Swedes, King Hygelac was killed, along with his son Heardred. Before their deaths, Beowulf remained loyal to his king and repeatedly led his army to victory. The king greatly rewarded him with treasure and a large estate on which he lived, and at the end of Hygelac's life Beowulf became king of the Geats. So Hrothgar's prediction came true. Beowulf reigned as king for half a century until his old age, when he met his death in the fiery breath of a dragon.

CONCLUSION

HOPE FOR THE FUTURE

Queen Wealhtheow and the priestess of Freyja both sought peace through their veneration of the Great Mother and their practice of compassion and mastery of seiðr, the ancient magic of that earlier hunter-gatherer age. King Hrothgar had hoped for peace, but he tried to attain it through physical strength, weaponry, and a powerful army. This benevolent king was open-handed in distributing his wealth, because he knew that the enemy of peace was greed. He found that his power over his foes was greater because of this benevolence, yet valuing power and strength is also the enemy of peace.

Though Hrothgar valued peace, since the time of his reign, and for the last twelve to thirteen hundred years since then, peace remains elusive. Wars continue, and the power of weapons escalates. We continue to rape and pillage our Great Mother Earth. To find the magic of seiðr we must give up our belief in the value of physical strength and power and our need to control others. We need to end our greed and the seeking of wealth. Giving up these values is the only way we can attain a world of peace, a world that will sustain us. The time is now, as we learn the teachings of the priestess of Freyja and the powers of seiðr.

Felicitas Goodman brought the powers of ecstatic trance to the attention of the world. Indeed, many are returning to venerating the Great Mother, seeking ways to heal and sustain her. In sustaining her, we sustain ourselves. There is hope; the present situation we find ourselves in is not hopeless. We can find peace, contentment, and sustainability; we can find Griðbustaðr in this life and the next; we can again find a world that Grendel could appreciate, a world in which he would have survived. So many species have disappeared since the time of Grendel, at a much faster rate now than ever before. Through seeing the earth from our center of harmony and observing as a cat stalks, we can find those ways that the earth and the flora and fauna that it sustains can survive. We have learned through ecstatic trance and the ecstatic postures that we can journey back in time to learn from our distant hunter-gatherer ancestors and revisit the Garden of Idunn. Though the garden will be different, we can find those ways to live sustainability to preserve our Great Mother. The groundwork was laid by Wealhtheow and Vanadisdottir for the Earth to continue. What they taught has not been forgotten in spite of the world being the way it is today.

These altered states of consciousness bring us in communion with our ancestors, our past lives, the people who live now, and with our Great Mother Earth with a telepathic awareness of what each knows and thinks, of how each lives. These altered states bring us into deep communion with everything around us, past and present, and with this deep understanding we can begin to attain a new sense of peace and contentment.

Many recognize that there will be great turmoil at this time; they recognize that change does not occur without such turmoil. It is important for us to recognize that the chaos that we see and experience around us is the death throes of the warrior world. Ervin Laszlo and Kingsley Dennis, authors of *Dawn of the Akashic Age: New Consciousness, Quantum Resonance, and the Future of the World,* give us until the year 2020 for this period of turmoil to pass.[1] If we survive the current time of transition, we will gain a new world of peace, a world that again can sustain us, a world that Queen Wealhtheow and Vanadisdottir, the priestess of Freyja believed in, a world that would have allowed Grendel and his kind to survive.

I have that hope.

NOTES

PROLOGUE.
A SHIFT ON OUR PLANET

1. Magaña, *2012–2021,* 138.
2. Ibid., 10.
3. Ibid., 15.
4. Ibid., 14.
5. Gebser, *Ever-Present Origin,* 297.
6. Laszlo, *Akashic Experience,* 250.
7. Gebser, *Ever-Present Origin,* 285.

INTRODUCTION.
THE PARADISE OF HUNTERS AND GATHERERS

1. Goodman, *Ecstasy, Ritual and Alternate Reality,* 17–18.
2. Quoted in Settegast, *Mona Lisa's Moustache,* 114.

CONCLUSION.
HOPE FOR THE FUTURE

1. Laszlo and Dennis, *Dawn of the Akashic Age,* 126–33.

GLOSSARY

Ægir: The god who held a feast to show off his new ale cauldron; the feast at which Loki insulted each of the gods and goddesses and killed Ægir's two servants, who were serving the ale.

Æsir: The race of warrior gods led by Odin that resides in Asgard.

Æðelstan: The son of King Gairvat who attempted to form a Danish settlement of East Anglia (England).

alant: The plant elecampane (*Inula helenium*), named by Idunn.

Anglia: The ancient name for England.

Angrboda: The mistress of Loki and the mother of Fenrir, Jormungand, and Hel.

Asgard: The domain of the Æsir in the upper world.

Asgerd: One of the five novices in training at the sacred tarn of Freyja.

ask: The name given the ash tree by Idunn, also known as the World Tree.

Astrid: One of the five novices in training at the sacred tarn of Freyja.

Athils: The king of the land of the Yngling, now known as Sweden.

Baldr: The most beautiful and gentle son of Odin and Frigg who dreamed of his own death, a death caused by the trickery of Loki; he returns after Ragnarǫk (the final battle between the gods and their adversaries) to become the god of gods.

baldrain: The name given to the valerian plant by Idunn.

bastu: A sauna.

berserkers: Warriors who work themselves into a frenzy before battle and are thought to be invulnerable.

Beow: The son of Scyld Scefing, the second great king of Denmark.

Beowulf: The Geat warrior and hero who rescued King Hrothgar by killing Grendel and his mother.

berberis: The berry bush barberry, named by Idunn.

Birka: Ancient trading center on a lake not far from what is now Stockholm.

Bor: The father of Odin, Vili and Ve, the son of Buri, the husband of Bestla, and the brother of Moðir.

Bragi: A son of Odin, the god of poetry, and the husband of Idunn.

Breca: The giant of a man who challenged other warriors in competition. He raced the Geat warrior Beowulf in swimming across the strait from Denmark to Scania, where he was rescued by Thord. Beowulf beat him in this race by swimming all the way to Finland.

Dan: The farm boy whose family was killed by the raiders of their farmstead. He was then fostered by the family of Thord.

Ecgtheow: The father of the Geat warrior Beowulf.

Elli: The giantess who in actuality is old age, as reported in the story of Utgard-Loki.

Erirk: A boy in one of Skald Bragason's stories of the young bully.

Fenrir: The wolf son of Loki who continued to grow to become a threat to the gods until it was restrained by a magical binding. This restraining of Fenrir cost Tyr his hand.

Forseti: The wise son of Baldr and Nanna, and the Vanir god of justice.

Forsetason: Earlier known as Thord, student of Vanadisdottir.

Freawaru: Daughter of Hrothgar and Wealhtheow who married Ingeld, the son of King Froda.

Freyja: The sister of Freyr and daughter of Njord. She is one of the fertility goddesses of the Vanir who went with her father to live with the Æsir.

Freyr: The brother of Freyja and the daughter of Njord. He is one of the fertility gods of the Vanir who went with his father to live with the Æsir.

Frigg: Odin's wife and mother of Baldr. She was originally of the Vanir.

Froda: The greedy king of the Heathobards, brother to King Healfdene, who in one story killed Healfdene and sought to kill Healfdene's three sons in order to become king.

Fyrstr: First—the horse Vanasdisdottir rode on her travels.

følfod: The plant coltsfoot.

Gæfuleysabjarg: The Cliff of Lucklessness, the place of residence in Freyja's domain of those warriors who die in their first battle. This cliff overlooks Harmagil, the Gorge of Sorrow, across which the warriors can see Gratabjǫð, the Weeping Fields, the place of women who die as virgins.

Gairvat: King of the Jutes, father of Æðelstan, who attempted to form a Nordic settlement in England.

Gefjon: The fertility goddess who plowed the land from Sweden to form the Danish island of Zealand. She was the wife of Scyld Scefing, the first king of Denmark, and is the caretaker of those women who die as virgins.

Gersemi: One of Freyja's two beautiful daughters.

Gratabjǫð: The Weeping Fields, the fields of Gefjon along Harmagil, the Gorge of Sorrow, where those women who die as virgins can see the warriors who die in their first battle.

Grendel: A creature from a previous hunter-gatherer age who became the tormentor of Hrothgar.

Griðbustaðr: The Dwelling Place of Peace, the place where those who understand and practice the compassionate magic of the Vanir reside after death.

Gudrid: One of the five novices in training at the sacred tarn of Freyja.

Gudvi: The young girl whose family and farm are destroyed by raiders, who was found by Thord and became another student of Vanadisdottir.

guldpil: The name given to the willow tree by Idunn.

Gunheid: King Olaf's wife and mother of Wealhtheow.

guvernante: Literally, "governess," also a teacher.

Hailgesson: King Olaf's first retainer, the leader chief of the king's warriors.

Halga: The youngest son of King Healfdene, the third king of Denmark.

Harmagil: The Gorge of Sorrow. From this gorge rises the smell of sulfur from Niflheim, the realm of those who die of illness and old age. It separates Gratabjǫð, the Weeping Fields, from Gæfuleysabjarg, the Cliff of Lucklessness.

hasselnöt: The Hazelnut tree.

Healfdall: Shepherd of King Hrothgar and student of Vanadisdottir.

Healfdene: The grandson of the first king of Denmark, Scyld Scefing, who became its third great king. He was the brother of King Frodi and had three sons, Heorogar, Hrothgar, and Halga, and a daughter, Signy. Hrothgar became the fourth and most powerful king of Denmark.

Heardred: The son of King Hygelac and Queen Hygd.

Heim: Thord's dog.

Heimdall: The Vanir god who chose to live with the Æsir who was given the position to guard Bifrost because of his acute hearing. He could hear the grass growing.

Hel: The daughter of Loki and Angrboda whom Odin threw into the underworld to care for those who died not of honor in battle but of illness and old age.

helgatjörn: Sacred forest pool or tarn.

Heorogar: The oldest son of the third king of Denmark, Healfdene, who died in battle in East Anglia (England).

Heorot: The great hall of King Hrothgar, named for the male red deer or hart.

Hildisvini: Freyja's boar, which she rode in battle.

hjulkrone: The plant borage, named by Idunn

Hleidargard: The royal seat of King Hrothgar on the Island of Zealand, now known as Gammel Lejre.

Hnoss: One of Freyja's two beautiful daughters.

Hrethric: The first son of Hrothgar and Wealhtheow.

Hreðel: Great king of the Geats, the father of King Hygelac.

Hring: King of Norway.

Hrothgar: The fourth and most powerful king of Denmark and the son of King Healfdene. His queen is Wealhtheow.

Hrothmund: The second son of Hrothgar and Wealhtheow.

Hrok: Son of Princess Signy, grandson of King Hrothgar.

Hugin: One of the ravens that sat on Odin's shoulder whispering in the ear of the god, bringing him the news of the nine worlds.

hvidtjørn: The name given to the plant hawthorn by Idunn.

hvidløg: The name given to the plant garlic.

hvilðgarðr: Literally, "the dwelling place of rest," the center of harmony within a person's body found just below the naval

Hygd: The wife and queen of King Hygelac.

Hygelac: King of the Geats whose champion is Beowulf.

Idunn: The Vanir goddess who kept the gods young by giving them golden apples from a tree in her garden and who taught the healing power of plants and trees. She was the wife of Bragi.

Inga: One of the five novices in training at the sacred tarn of Freyja.

Ingeld: The son of the Heathobard king Froda, who married Hrothgar's daughter Freawaru.

Jarl Sævil: The husband of Signy, daughter of the Danish king Healfdene.

Jormungand: The serpent son of Loki and Angrboda whom Odin threw into the ocean, where it grew to surround Midgard to hold its own tail in its mouth.

Jotunheim: The domain in Midgard that is the realm of the giants.

Jotunn: The Old Norse word for giant.

Juteland: The Danish peninsula north of Germany and to the west of Zealand.

kamille: The name given the plant chamomile by Idunn.

kongelys: The plant mullein.

kulsukker: The name given the plant comfrey by Idunn

Kvasir: The wisest of the gods who first brewed mead from the spittle of the gods, the drink of the gods. He is also the god of the Vanir who was offered in exchange for Mimir of the Æsir to ensure peace between the Vanir and the Æsir.

Liknvi: The mother who lost one son killed in battle and goes to Wealhtheow and Vanadisdottir because of her concern about her other son becoming a warrior.

Loki: The trickster god skilled in shape-shifting and the father of Jormungand, Fenrir, and Hel. His confrontations of the gods because of their hypocrisy led to his restraint until the time of Ragnarǫk, the final battle that brings an end to the world. He is the cause of earthquakes.

Lokison: A boy in one of Skald Bradison's stories of a young bully.

martrem: The plant feverfew, named by Idunn.

Midgard: The middle world; our world as we know it.

Mjollnir: The hammer of Thor that causes lightning when thrown by Thor and then returns to his hand.

mjoðr: The name given to the honey drink, mead.

Moðir: The Great Mother, the mother of the Vanir. She is the sister of Bor who is the father of Odin, thus she is Odin's aunt. She is the daughter of Buri, the mother of Njord, and the grandmother of Freyja and Freyr. Her husband is Slœgr, the creative one.

Munin: One of Odin's ravens that sits on his shoulder, bringing him the news of the nine worlds.

mynte: The name given to the plant mint that is used for tea.

Nanna: Baldr's wife and one of the Vanir.

Niflheim: The realm of those who die of illness and old age, which is ruled by Hel.

Njord: The god of the Vanir and father of Freyr and Freyja. He is the god of the wind and sea who married the giantess Skaði.

nœlde: The name given the plant nettles by Idunn.

Nöttgangr: A name give to Forsetason by Olaf's retainers, meaning "Nightwalker."

Nydagan: The New Dawn, the birth of the new age of time-free transparency that is beginning now in the twenty-first century.

Odr: Freyja's wandering husband.

Odin: The father of the gods, father of Thor.

Olaf: King of Scania whose daughter is Wealhtheow. His queen is Gunheid.

Olfdene: Banished son of King Olaf, brother of Wealhtheow, who dies in battle in East Anglia.

perikon: The name given to the plant St. John's wort by Idunn.

purpur-solhat: The name given the plant echinacea by Idunn.

Ragnarǫk: The final battle between the gods and their adversaries that brings an end to the world and the rebirth of Baldr.

rejnfang: The name given to the plant tansy by Idunn.

rönn: The mountain ash tree.

Scyld Scefing: The first king of Denmark and the husband of the goddess Gefjon.

seiðr: The magic of the Vanir.

seiðhjallr: The platform on which volvas (shamans) sit that allows them to see or journey into the future.

seiðmaðr: A man who practices seiðr.

Signy: The daughter of the Danish king Healfdene who married Jarl Sævil, brother to Hrothgar and Halga. Her son is Hrok, and Fiona is her guvernante.

Sigrid: The queen of Healafdene, mother of Signy.

Sigyn: Loki's wife, who remained faithful to him until the end. When Loki was restrained with a poisonous snake hanging over his head, Sigyn protected him by catching the dripping poison in a bowl.

skald: A poet or bard who composes in the courts of the Nordic kings.

Skaði: The daughter of the giant Thiazi and the wife of Njord.

Skjǫldung: One of the major ancient tribes of Nordic people of Denmark and Southern Sweden, centered in what is now Gammel Lejre, Denmark

Slœgr: A giant whose name means "the creative one," who is the husband of Moðir and the father of Njord.

Thiazi: The giant who kidnapped Idunn, who afterward was rescued by the shape-shifting powers of Loki. Thiazi was killed in a fire in Asgard.

Thokk: A giant thought to be Loki in disguise who prevented Baldr's return from Hel.

Thor: The son of Odin whose mother is Fjorgyn. He is the husband of Sif. This warrior god brings lightning and thunder with the throw of his hammer.

Thord: The disfigured farm boy who was trained in seiðr by Vanadisdottir. He was given the new name of Forsetason.

Tora: One of the five novices in training at the sacred tarn of Freyja.

Tyr: The son of Odin and the god of war who sacrificed his hand in order to restrain Fenrir the wolf.

Ullr: The Vanir god of archery and skiing, the creative and inventive son of Njord and Siff, and the grandson of Moðir.

Unferth: An honored champion of King Hrothgar who sat at the head of the king's table of warriors.

Utgard-Loki: The giant skilled in deception who repeatedly tricked Thor.

Valhalla: The realm in the upper world presided over by Odin that becomes the home of those who die valiantly in battle.

Valkyries: The beautiful women who escort those who die valiantly in battle to Valhalla.

Vanaheim: The upper world realm of the Vanir.

Vanir: The race of fertility gods and goddesses that predated the Æsir. Because of their magical powers in battle, their battles with the physical powerful Æsir were stalemates.

Vanadisdottir: Meaning "daughter of Freyja"; a priestess of Freyja. While in trance, I heard the ancient stories recorded in the book from this priestess; she is the guvernante of Wealhtheow.

Vänern: The lake that resulted when Gefjon plowed the land to form the Danish island of Zealand.

Vättern: The lake that was formed when Freyja, while searching for her husband, Odr, pulled on the reins of the boar Hildisvini, causing the boar to put his butt down as he skidded to a stop, digging the long trench that formed this lake.

Var: The goddess of oath-taking who listens to the vows of marriage.

vejbred: The plant plantain, named by Idunn.

volva: A seeress or shaman and practitioner of seiðr.

Wealhtheow: Queen to King Hrothgar, daughter of King Olaf and Queen Gunheid, sister of Olfdene.

Wulfgar: A member of King Hrothgar's court who escorted Beowulf and his men to stand before the king.

Yggdrasill: The World Tree, whose roots are in the upper, middle, and lower worlds.

Ynglings: One of the major ancient tribes of Nordic people of Sweden, based in what is now Gammel Uppsala, Sweden.

BIBLIOGRAPHY

Anderson, Gunnar, Lena Beronius Jörpeland, Jan Duner, Sara Fritsch, and Eva Skylberg. *Att föra gudarnas talan*. Stockholm, Sweden: Riksantikvarieämbetet, 2004.

Braden, Gregg. *The Divine Matrix: Bridging Time, Space, Miracles, and Belief.* Carlsbad, Calif.: Hay House, 2007.

Brink, Nicholas E. *Baldr's Magic: The Power of Norse Shamanism and Ecstatic Trance.* Rochester, Vt.: Bear and Co., 2014.

———. *The Power of Ecstatic Trance: Practices for Healing, Spiritual Growth, and Accessing the Universal Mind.* Rochester, Vt.: Bear and Co., 2013.

Calleman, Carl Johan. *The Mayan Calendar and the Transformation of Consciousness.* Rochester, Vt.: Bear and Co., 2004.

Chambers, R. W. *Beowulf: An Introduction to the Study of the Poem.* Cambridge, UK: Cambridge University Press, 1959.

Clow, Barbara Hand. *The Mayan Code: Time Acceleration and Awakening the World Mind.* Rochester, Vt.: Bear and Co., 2007.

Coles, John. *Shadows of the Northern Past: Rock Carvings of Bohuslän and Østfold.* Oxford, UK: Oxbow Books, 2005.

Deloria Jr., Vine. *The World We Used to Live In: Remembering the Powers of the Medicine Men.* Golden, Colo.: Fulcrum, 2006.

Gebser, Jean. *The Ever-Present Origin.* Translated by Noel Barstad. Athens: Ohio University Press, 1953.

Goodman, Felicitas. *Ecstasy, Ritual, and Alternate Reality: Religion in a*

Pluralistic World. Bloomington: Indiana University Press, 1990.

———. *Where the Spirits Ride the Wind: Trance Journeys and Other Ecstatic Experiences.* Bloomington: Indiana University Press, 1990.

Gore, Belinda. *Ecstatic Body Postures: An Alternate Reality Workbook.* Rochester, Vt.: Bear and Co., 1995.

———. *The Ecstatic Experience: Healing Postures for Spirit Journeys.* Rochester, Vt.: Bear and Co., 2009.

Laszlo, Ervin. *The Akashic Experience: Science and the Cosmic Memory Field.* Rochester, Vt.: Inner Traditions, 2009.

———. *Science and the Akashic Field: An Integral Theory of Everything.* Rochester, Vt.: Inner Traditions, 2007.

Laszlo, Ervin, and Kingsley L. Dennis. *Dawn of the Akashic Age: New Consciousness, Quantum Resonance, and the Future of the World.* Rochester, Vt.: Inner Traditions, 2013.

Magaña, Sergio. *2012–2021: The Dawn of the Sixth Sun: The Path of Quetzalcoatl.* Torino, Italy: Blossoming Books, 2012.

Radin, Dean. *Entangled Minds: Extrasensory Experiences in a Quantum Reality.* New York: Paraview Pocket Books, 2006.

Settegast, Mary. *Mona Lisa's Moustache: Making Sense of a Dissolving World.* Grand Rapids, Mich.: Phanes Press, 2001.

Sheldrake, Rupert. *The Presence of the Past: Morphic Resonance and the Habits of Nature.* Rochester, Vt.: Park Street Press, 1995.

Tarnas, Richard. *Cosmos and Psyche: Intimations of a New World View.* New York: Penguin Books, 2006.

Wright, David, trans. *Beowulf: A Prose Translation.* New York: Penguin, 1957.

INDEX

Number in *italics* indicate illustrations.

228

BOOKS OF RELATED INTEREST

Baldr's Magic
The Power of Norse Shamanism and Ecstatic Trance
by Nicholas E. Brink, Ph.D.

The Power of Ecstatic Trance
Practices for Healing, Spiritual Growth, and Accessing the Universal Mind
by Nicholas E. Brink, Ph.D.

Norse Goddess Magic
Trancework, Mythology, and Ritual
by Alice Karlsdóttir

The Ecstatic Experience
Healing Postures for Spirit Journeys
by Belinda Gore

Shaking Medicine
The Healing Power of Ecstatic Movement
by Bradford Keeney

Shamanic Breathwork
Journeying beyond the Limits of the Self
by Linda Star Wolf

Seven Secrets of Time Travel
Mystic Voyages of the Energy Body
by Von Braschler

Shapeshifting
Techniques for Global and Personal Transformation
by John Perkins

INNER TRADITIONS • BEAR & COMPANY
P.O. Box 388
Rochester, VT 05767
1-800-246-8648
www.InnerTraditions.com

Or contact your local bookseller